CHRISTIAN MARRIAGE:
Grace and Work

CHRISTIAN MARRIAGE
Grace & Work

ROBERT E. MONEY

BROADMAN PRESS
NASHVILLE, TENNESSEE

Unless otherwise noted, all Scripture quotations are from the *Revised Standard Version of the Bible,* copyrighted 1946,1952, © 1971, 1973. Used by permission.

Scripture quotations marked (KJV) are from the *King James Version of the Bible.*

Scripture quotations marked (NASB) are from the *New American Standard Bible.* © The Lockman Foundation, 1960, 1962, 1963, 1968, 1971, 1972, 1973, 1975, 1977. Used by permission.

Scripture quotations marked (Phillips) are reprinted with permission of MacMillan Publishing Co., Inc. from J. B. Phillips: *The New Testament in Modern English,* Revised Edition. © J. B. Phillips 1958, 1960, 1972.

Library of Congress Cataloging-in-Publication Data
Money, Robert E. 1937-
  Christian marriage : grace and work / Robert E. Money.
  p. cm.
  ISBN: 0-8054-3004-0
  1. Marriage--Religious aspects--Christianity. I. Title.
BV835.M65 1991
248.4--dc20

89-28939
CIP

To my family:

My wife, Sydnor, who is the friend who "knows me as I am, understands where I've been, accepts who I've become, and still invites me to grow" (source unknown);

My children, Bob, Meredith, and Jeff, each unique, special, and irreplaceable;

My parents, Joe and Lula Money, who gave me the roots with which to grow;

My wife's parents, J. B. and Eugenia Aiken, who gave me the wings to fly in a new and different direction.

Preface

When I was a student in clinical pastoral education at North Carolina Baptist Hospital in Winston-Salem, North Carolina, I chose as a part of my clinical program to meet the requirements of Wake Forest University for a master's degree in pastoral counseling. For this degree I had to write a thesis in which I was required to choose a subject that would interface theology and psychology. I chose adolescence as my subject. (The impressive title, one of the requirements of academia, was *H. Richard Niebuhr's Concept of the Responsible Self as Related to the Psychosocial Need for Emotional Independence in Adolescence and Its Implications for Pastoral Counseling with Adolescents!*)

More in retrospect than in forethought, my decision to research and write a thesis on adolescence was no mere happenstance. My adolescence was very significant to me. Even though I came through it without trauma or major crisis, I went through something I did not understand. My adult life has been so bound to those years that I wanted to theoretically and academically walk back through them as a way to walk better through my adulthood. Not only was my subject an interesting choice; it was a wise one.

As a married person and as a pastoral counselor who focuses heavily on the marriage relationship, I felt the same need to better understand marriage. That need for myself and for others prompted me to research marriage theologically and psychologically. More importantly, it caused me to want to share my growing understanding of marriage as seen from the perspective of my own marital experience and from those with whom I work. I have been given the privilege of seeing many marriages openly. This book's voice comes from many marriages: some broken, some in crisis, and some growing by the partners' deliberate choice, dedicated to making good marriages better.

The title of the book, *Christian Marriage: Grace and Work,* reflects the critical need to recognize both the relational needs and the functional needs inherent in a marriage. Using the biblical model of marriage, the relational needs are established as primary and the functional needs as secondary. Both are valid and complement each other in the same way that salvation is shown by both grace and works.

The central chapters in the book present five distinguishable characteristics that can be evaluated and scored as to whether a marriage tends to be more relational or functional. A relational marriage tends to score high on all of the relational characteristics and a functional marriage on all of the functional needs. Continuity is the rule rather than the exception.

These five marital characteristics were chosen by my wife and me as we were preparing to lead a Sunday evening marriage enrichment event for some fifteen couples who had responded to a general churchwide invitation. We have used these characteristics for several years without feeling the need to either add to them or delete them. They have proven themselves sufficient.

As you read the book, let me encourage you not to be so intent on finding quick answers for your specific marital need or situation. Rather, read with a desire to find a new insight and with a freedom to soar beyond where you are in marriage to higher, better, and deeper experiences in marriage. God created marriage as a gift. It is inexhaustible in terms of its possibilities, untapped in terms of its resources, and unused in terms of its vast benefits. In its purpose, marriage is both special and irreplaceable.

I am grateful to First Baptist Church, Knoxville, Tennessee, for the commitment and vision to create a minister of family life staff position. The church supports and encourages a family life program that is one of both intervention and prevention. My church family planted a rare and different seed, watered and fed it, pruned it, and caused it to flourish. The fruits have been shared by many.

Swan Haworth, my mentor and friend, modeled for me the roles of pastor and counselor, and he was a primary resource for me in establishing my own identity as a pastoral counselor. His person, as well as his ideas and theories, permeate this writing.

My secretary, Barbara Phillips, is a partner in ministry who cares enough to be persistent and patient with a manuscript that "grows as it changes and changes as it grows."

Contents

Guided Instructions

In these pages you will find a self-contained marriage enrichment opportunity. Marriage enrichment is an approach to marriage in which couples are helped to identify growth areas. It is the primary purpose of marriage enrichment to help couples make good marriages better.

This particular approach is focused on "Christian Marriage: Grace and Work." The first two chapters clearly define the approach. The third chapter gives particular insight into the first hour of marriage enrichment or counseling. Five chapters follow that deal with five basic marital needs. After each of the chapters, several exercises are included to help couples determine how specific needs are being addressed in their marriage. Use the exercises to seek new insight, to encourage conversation with your spouse, and to guide you toward marital enrichment. The final chapter is collected data. Use it to compare your own marital growth with seventy other couples.

After experiencing this enrichment opportunity, invite others to join you for a group experience. Ask your pastor, a staff member, a layperson, or a couple to lead the group in using the material. Request that each couple read the book before participation in the enrichment event.

Marriage is God's good gift to us. Commitment is its strength; growth is its assurance.

1

Marriage Defined

Marriage is a word dressed in so many garments that to talk about it demands that we define it. One way to define it is to identify its outward boundaries, from negative to positive, from realistic to idealistic, from practical to romantic. Robert Winch stated that "in courtship, two people present personalities they have tailored to fit the moment. It is when their masks come off, the marriage really begins."[1] Anne Morrow Lindbergh said that a

> good relationship has a pattern like a dance and is built on some of the same rules. The partners do not need to hold on tightly because they move confidently in the same pattern, intricate but gay and swift and free, like a country dance of Mozart's. There is no place here for the possessive clutch, the clinging arm, the heavy hand, only the barest touch in passing. Now arm in arm, now face to face, now back to back, it does not matter which. Because they know they are partners moving to the same rhythm, creating a pattern together and being invisibly nourished by it.

Marriage as understood and experienced by most people is somewhere in between.

As a marriage counselor, I soon discovered that many couples are participating in a relationship about which they have limited definition and understanding. When they come for counseling—just as they go to a physician—they expect both diagnosis and prognosis in the first visit. They need and demand some definition. They are in something that is not working efficiently. They are focused more on the pain, the tension, and the symptoms; and they have little understanding of the nature, the need, and the meaning of the marital relationship. They approach their marriage much as they would their car. As long as it works, fine. When it fails to work, the problem is identified by the smell, the sight, or the sound of the nonfunctioning part. The failure to understand the car and to care for the car is ignored by the pressing need to fix the ailing part and get the car going again. The car is fixed but not understood.

I soon learned that distressed couples need to understand what they are doing in marriage so that they can get beyond symptoms and parts and conceptually, at least, understand the nature and meaning of marriage—the whole. In the initial hour of marital counseling, I seek to help a couple to conceptually understand what it is they are about in marriage.

In marriage enrichment, the initial task is the same. Couples who are either slightly or strongly interested in marital enrichment need a definition, a clear mental picture of what marriage is and what it means. Most persons seem to enter into marriage swept along by the strong currents of emotional needs, or with some rather vague notions about marriage based on parental or other models. Or they get married with such a comfortable idea about marriage that they quickly find themselves swimming in waters that seem familiar but are not understood. Herein lies a basic life principle: People cannot and do not change what they do not understand.

In the initial session, whether it is marital counseling

or marital enrichment, whether it is one couple or several couples, it is critical that a couple (couples) and counselor (leader) establish a clear, workable definition of marriage. I have found it most helpful to use a visual image that takes the abstract or theory and makes it concrete and practical. On a board I draw the following figure and state, "This is my definition of marriage."

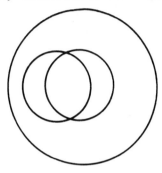

In marriage, two persons make a dual commitment. They make a commitment to the institution of marriage, the outer circle, and they make a commitment to a person, the inner circle. A good marriage needs both. A commitment to the institution without a commitment to the growth of the relationship creates marital boredom and personal vulnerabilities. A commitment to the relationship without a growing commitment to the institution is unromantic, unrealistic, and unwise.

A history of marriage demonstrates that in the more traditional marriages of the 1920s, thirties, forties, and fifties, the commitment to the institution was primary, and the commitment to the relationship was secondary. The duties and functions of the marriage were far more important than the growth and enrichment of the relationship. It was the very nature of marriage to create and produce a family in which the duties and functions required to care for that family were primary. Since the family did not assign those tasks to outside agencies and organizations, the demands of those tasks were often viewed and understood as more essential and more important to marriage than the relationship of the couple. For others, those family tasks either quickly overwhelmed or slowly supplanted the romantic or intentional desire to keep the relationship primary.

In the 1960s and 1970s, a period of history characterized by a rebellious spirit of anti-institutionalism, relationships were elevated to the primary position, and institutional tasks and functions were demoted to a much less important position. Since social correction is usually addressed and changed by employing radical and extreme means, youth viewed institutions as not only unessential to life but as barriers and bullies to life as it could and was meant to be. Thus their attitude was, "If you feel it, do it; if love is present, all else is right with the world." In their extreme way, they sought to breathe life back into a dead or dying corpse. Though extreme in origin, the effect of their efforts was often like leaven in dough. Every strata of society was penetrated, marriage and the family in particular. In the years that followed, the relationship in marriage became elevated to primary status, and the marital institution was demoted to a secondary position. The result is that in today's understanding of marriage, there is a growing need and understanding to view marriage as both institution and relationship, each needing the presence and support of the other.

A biblical perspective of marriage illustrates this need to join the institution and the relationship. The best and clearest biblical model is the analogy of how God chose to relate to His people. In the Old Testament, the relationship between God and Israel is a familiar marital model that is used to reveal, to inform, and to correct. Marriage, in the New Testament, is employed to demonstrate and illustrate the growing, developing relationship between Christ and the church.

In a biblical understanding of marriage, there is a growing understanding of God's intention and purpose for marriage. In revelation there are two vital elements. First, our seeking does not reveal God. It opens us to receive what He reveals. Secondly, God has chosen to relate His revelation to our readiness and willingness to receive. In regard to a biblical understanding of marriage and the family, the Old Testament sets forth the creation of an institution that in theory is full and complete, but in practice is developing. In the New Testament, the theory is present in complete form and model: Christ the bridegroom and the church as the bride.

Historically in the American culture, marriage has been highly influenced by the Bible. The Old Testament model, referred to as the institutional model, has exerted the greater influence. In this model the roles and duties are more critical to marriage than the growth and enrichment of the relationship. In today's society, however, relationships are becoming more important to the stability and permanence of the marriage. The critical issue here is that the duties and functions of an institutional marriage are more clearly defined and understood than are the needs of a relational marriage. The preferred marital choice today is a relational one, yet the understanding and preparation for that choice are severely lacking. The very things couples prefer, want, and expect too frequently are not being produced.

One of the reasons for that is in the American society we are educated, both by model and instruction, to perform a function, to fulfill a duty, to do a job. We receive limited guidance, either by models or by instructions, to know how to be relational. Couples today choose the relational style of marriage but with limited understanding as to what it requires or how it is done.

It is true that more marriages end in divorce today than ever before. It is natural and right for church staff and members to be concerned by this trend. The church can respond to the fears created by divorce statistics and to the obvious changes that are occurring in marriage in one of three ways.

First, the church can march with the growing band of those who demand that marriage return to the ways of "the fathers"—the traditional style of marriage in which duties and roles are clearly defined and persons are bound and limited by them—to the institution that is honored and preserved at all cost. This model is characterized by defined roles and functions and often by male dominance and female submission. For some, this has been and will continue to be their choice, and it can and does work; but it has severe limitations. This style tends to opt for security and stability at the expense of growth and intimacy.

The second option is that of "thoroughly modern Millie" in which marriage is excessively relational. The relationship of the couple is so primary that the institution often is viewed as an enemy that stalks, captures, and kills. Love is supreme, and how the partners feel about each other is all-important.

The third option is what I call the biblical model. It is the old covenant fulfilled in the new one. The new covenant does not discard or disregard the old covenant. It completes it. It takes the form and gives it new and better substance. Jesus did not discard or disregard the old covenant. He said, "I did not come to abolish [the old], but to fulfill" (Matt. 5:17, NASB). At the same time, He warned, "No one puts new wine into old wineskins" (Luke 5:37,

NASB). He certainly did not imply that wineskins were not needed. He confirmed that just as the substance changes, the form must also change. The biblical model of marriage to which I subscribe is one that is both institutional and relational. It is the blending of the old and the new into something richer and better and greater.

Institutional

In all settings, institutions are created and preserved to serve the welfare of humanity. They are means to an end. In an institutional model, the institution becomes more important than the person(s) it serves. It ceases to be a means and becomes an end. One biblical example of an institution that was created for the welfare and good of human beings is the sabbath. Remember Jesus said, "The sabbath [the institution] was made for man, and not man for the sabbath [the institution]" (Mark 2:27, KJV).

The institution of marriage, historically understood, has several basic purposes:

1. To provide a setting in which children can be born and raised under conditions best structured to take care of their needs and to enhance their opportunity to grow up to become mature, responsible adults;

2. To keep the creative, urgent, and dynamic impulse of sex under some kind of control so that it can be used as a good, productive force within society;

3. To make possible the unique relationship between a man and a woman that nurtures within each of them the potential to discover and express the best and deepest within each. A lifetime of living and sharing is the best context in which that can occur.

In the Old Testament the marriage relationship between God and Israel is often affirmed. Hosea, speaking

for God, said, "I will betroth you to me for ever; I will betroth you to me in righteousness and in justice, in steadfast love, and in mercy" (Hos. 2:19-20, KJV). Ezekiel expressed it this way: "When I passed by you again and
looked upon you, behold, you were at the age for love; and
I spread my skirt over you, and covered your nakedness:
yea, I plighted my troth to you and entered into a covenant with you, says the Lord God, and you became mine"
(Ezek. 16:8-14).

God and Israel established a mutual covenant, a nup-
tial agreement. In their covenant, their marriage, the institution was valid and necessary, but Israel made a critical mistake. In substituting the institutional functions
for the personal relationship, Israel unwittingly caused
the marriage to become more and more one of form and
duty. With time, the joys of the relationship diminished,
and Israel gave allegiance to a hollow form that had less
and less meaning. She continued to take seriously her
functions and duties, but she neglected to nurture the relationship. Israel, blind to what was happening, felt safe
and secure in her institution. She was the favored one,
chosen and special. It was a permanent arrangement.
God spoke, but Israel did not listen:

Has the Lord as great delight in burnt offerings and
sacrifices,
as in obeying the voice of the Lord?
Behold to obey is better than sacrifice,
and to hearken than the fat of rams (1 Sam. 15:22).

David, broken inside because of his estranged relationship with God, cried,
"For thou hast no delight in sacrifice;
were I to give a burnt offering, thou wouldst not be
pleased.
The sacrifice acceptable to God is a broken spirit;

a broken and contrite heart [a restored relationship]"
(Ps. 51:17).

"For I desire a steadfast love and not sacrifice,
the knowledge of God, rather than burnt offerings"
(Hos. 6:6).

God acted, but Israel did not see. As Hosea pursued Go-
mer and would not let her go, God pursued Israel and
would not let her go. "How can I give you up, O Ephraim!/
How can I hand you over, O Israel!" (Hos. 11:8).

Israel allowed her marital security to change from one
of being highly invested in a faithful, growing relationship to one that was determined by the selection itself. To
be chosen by God became more and more important to
Israel, and to be in a mutual covenant with God became
less and less important. A false sense of security offered
Israel privilege without responsibility, form without substance, status without service and submission. It changed
a mutually meaningful relationship into a hollow, sepul-
chral institution.

In the institutional marriage today, duties and functions are primary; personal and marital growth are secondary. Children are taught best how to succeed, but they
receive little guidance in how to relate to others. Belonging is earned by hard work, and grace is often so neglected
it is almost nonexistent. In marriage, the institution is
the form but not the substance; it is the container but not
the ingredient; it is the frame but not the picture. Yet
substance without form, ingredients without containers,
and pictures without frames are limited, incomplete, and
unmanageable. It is true that institutions were made for
people. But they were made!

Joe and Edna had been married for fifteen years. Both
had grown up in traditional homes where marriages were
understood as being institutional. The institution was

strong and intact, providing the children with an unques-
tioned sense of security. The relational needs of the family were less obvious and often went unmet; thus the couple viewed relational needs as less valid and important.

Both Joe and Edna functioned well in their marriage,
which was much like their parents' marriages. The commitment to marriage, on one hand, freed them from the
fear of divorce and allowed them to pursue and fulfill
their prescribed functions and duties well. On the other
hand, their marriage was continuously being injected
with a drug that caused them to be maritally anesthe-
tized to their relational needs. Edna was strongly into her
functional roles as saleswoman, mother, and wife, while
Joe was slowly acknowledging his relational needs for a
partner and a companion. He began to verbalize his
needs, softly at first, then loudly, and finally thunderous-
ly. Although Edna heard him, she ignored his needs.
When Joe announced to Edna that he was through with
the marriage and wanted out, she entered a state of
shock. Edna had felt so secure within the marital institution that she could not imagine its ending. She never acknowledged that Joe had relational needs that the institution of marriage could not meet. Her marriage ended in
divorce while Edna was still at a loss to figure out what
had happened.

From a biblical perspective, marital security is not to
be found in the love of law but in the higher law of love.

Relational

Beginning in the late fifties and continuing on to the
present, in reaction to the limits and boredom created by
the institutional marriage, a new style of marriage frequently referred to as the relational marriage has
emerged. Dr. David Mace has observed that in the old

form of marriage, the institutional form, the central goal of marriage was familial obligations and duties. Personal fulfillment was peripheral.[2]

In the midst of change, extremes are always potentially present. This was true for many couples. The relationship was not only primary; it was viewed synonymously with marriage.

In the New Testament there is a new model that grows out of the old. Christ is the bridegroom, and the church is His bride. The marriage occurred through a commitment of faith. For Christ, the church became His bride as He loved her sacrificially. He nourished, cherished, and purified her (Eph. 5:25-26,29). The church responded to Him with reverence and obedience, in faithfulness in renouncing every other husband, in desiring and seeking purity and holiness (Eph. 5:21,24,27,31). (See the *International Dictionary of the Bible*.) A personal, growing relationship between Christ and the church, between Christ and each member, was both critical and central. Yet that personal relationship was related significantly to the institution: the church. In the old covenant, Israel's being chosen by God became a substitute for a personal, living relationship with God. In the new covenant, "knowing Christ" personally was both entry into the community of believers and the living vitality of the Christian pilgrimage and journey. In Him the church was both called and empowered to infest the world with a transforming, creative love as the following passages illustrate:

> Abide in me, and I in you. As the branch cannot bear fruit by itself, unless it abides in the vine, neither can you, unless you abide in me. I am the vine, you are the branches. He who abides in me, and I in him, he it is that bears much fruit (John 15:4-5).

If any one is in Christ, he is a new creation; the old has passed away, behold, the new has come (2 Cor. 5:17).

Go therefore and make disciples of all nations, baptizing them in the name of the Father and of the Son and of the Holy Spirit, teaching them to observe all that I have commanded you; and lo, I am with you always (Matt. 28:19-20).

A personal faith in which one knows and is known by Christ is essential; yet a personal faith does not stand alone, all-sufficient. It needs the church as a context in which to nourish and practice that faith.

A Relational/Functional Marriage

Meaningful relationships have a need for the institution. The biblical model of marriage most clearly focused in the relationships between God and Israel and Christ and the church is neither the institutional model nor the relational model. The biblical model here is one in which there is a dual commitment. There is a personal commitment, and there is a commitment to an institution: marriage.

In the Old Testament model of marriage, God enjoyed Israel, and Israel delighted in her relationship with God. There was a spontaneous, creative joy that spilled forth out of the relationship.

Make a joyful noise to the Lord, . . .
Serve the Lord with gladness!
Come into his presence with singing!

Know that the Lord is God!
. . . .

For the Lord is good;
his steadfast love endures for ever
and his faithfulness to all generations (Ps. 100).

I will be as the dew to Israel;
he shall blossom as the lily,
he shall strike root as the poplar,
his shoots shall spread out;
his beauty shall be like the olive,
and his fragrance like Lebanon.
They shall return and dwell beneath my shadow,
they shall flourish as a garden;
they shall blossom as the vine,
their fragrance shall be like the wine of Lebanon (Hos.
14:5-7).

Then there were the duties and functions of responsible
living. The covenant was based on mutual trust, faithfulness, and responsibility.

> If you [Israel] will obey my voice and keep my cove-
> nant, you shall be my own possession among all peo-
> ples; for all the earth is mine, and you shall be to me a
> kingdom of priests and a holy nation (Ex. 19:5-6).

> He has showed you, O man [Israel], what is good;
> and what does the Lord require of you
> but to do justice, and to love kindness,
> and to walk humbly with your God? (Mic. 6:8).

The Old Testament model is one that reveals and supports the dual commitment. The covenant between God
and Israel involved both a being and a doing.

In the New Testament model, the dual commitment remains firm. The primary difference between the Old Testament model and the New Testament model is the em-
phasis that is placed upon the personal versus the
national relationship. The covenant is between a person
and God, couched in and nurtured by the community of
faith: the church. To Nicodemus, Jesus said, "Unless one
is born anew, he cannot see the kingdom of God" (John
3:3). In the lengthy dialogue between Jesus and the woman at the well, she thought nationally, and he thought

personally. She said for years her ancestors had worshiped on Mount Gerizim, "and you say that in Jerusalem is the place where men ought to worship" (John 4:20). Jesus personalized worship by saying to her that the place is not the critical factor. The key to worship is one's life. It has to do with a person's intentions and desire for truth (see John 4:1-30).

In the New Covenant, a personal faith was both the entrance into and the way of a new and growing relationship. Still there was the need for the structured community. For Jesus, it was the inner core of twelve disciples and the larger band of faithful followers. The forming church of Jesus' life and ministry became the established church of His postresurrection. Paul, writing out of his own personal encounter, stated that because of his sincere but misdirected past, he was of all people the most unfit to be an apostle. It was not his works but God's grace that corrected and freed Paul to say, "But by the grace of God I am what I am" (1 Cor. 15:10). Paul took his personal faith by grace and worked it out in the community of faith. The body does not consist of one member but of many. Just as the body needs each of its parts, so does the body of Christ: the church. "You are the body of Christ and individually members of it" (1 Cor. 12:27). In the New Testament the covenant is a personal commitment lived out in a community of faith.

In a Christian marriage today, the institution is needed to provide stability and assurance when the marital relationship is strained and conflictual. The marital institution needs the developing, growing life of the marital relationship to keep it active, changing, and from becoming hollow and dead.

When I was a small boy growing up in south Alabama,

we had pecan trees on our farm. The trees were not planted in groves as some were in the area, but they grew naturally and singly all around the homeplace. Dad was very gracious with the pecans, both in terms of letting us eat all we wanted and letting us sell them to earn extra money for things we wanted. Sometimes, when finances were tight, the money from the sale of the pecans was used for family needs and essentials.

In the fall, when the pecans matured, they would slowly separate from their green hulls. With the aid of the wind or from the jarring applied by a strong foot on the individual limbs, the pecans would fall to the ground. Sometimes we gathered them after we had forced them to fall. Other times we gathered them after they had chosen to fall or when they were aided by the natural elements of wind and rain.

I recall the ecstasy I felt when I found a spot where the pecans seemed to collect as if they were members of a family. It was so much easier to fill my bucket and then empty it into the bulging gunnysack (burlap bag)!

One of the things I learned early about pecans was that I was not the only one interested in them. When I picked one up, I would often find a pecan that looked good at first glance but was no longer good. A small worm had bored its way through the hull, had enjoyed a good meal, and had exited out of the same hole it had entered. The hull was left intact, but the meat was all gone! If I missed seeing the hole, what appeared to be a good pecan was added to the bucket and poured into the sack. If I saw the tiny hole, I had several options: I left it on the ground; I picked it up and threw it away; or I pressed it against a good pecan in my hand and felt the hull crumble into bits, which I then threw away with some disappointment and anger.

Herein lies a good analogy. A healthy pecan has both a strong hull and a full, firm kernel. A good marriage is both institutional (hull) and relational (kernel). The kernel needs the hull, and the hull is the strength and protection for the kernel. A pecan needs both.

For the Christian, relationship with God is primary, but the need for the institution, the church, is essential. So it is in marriage. In the presence of God and friends a couple makes a commitment to a relationship that grows as it changes and changes as it grows. The couple also makes a commitment to the institution of marriage, which protects, supports, and nurtures that growth by offering definition, stability, and security. A good marriage needs both substance and form.

Roles and Responsibilities

In marriage, couples take on new roles and responsibilities while maintaining old ones. These roles, the old ones and the new ones, are vital, both personally and maritally. They make demands on our time and energy. In marriage the roles would look something like this:

husband	couple	wife
son	husband	daughter
grandson	wife	granddaughter
brother	son-in-law	sister
uncle	daughter-in-law	aunt
grandfather	provider	grandmother
engineer	parent	lawyer
		friend

Some of these roles are acquired with marriage while others are premarriage. Marriage does not diminish their importance, but marriage does assign them secondary positions. Thus a husband and a wife leave their parents and commit to each other. The husband/wife relationship is secondary only to our relationship with God, and that itself is complimentary—not conflictual—when properly understood and kept.

From a marital perspective, roles can be viewed very differently. In marriages that tend to be more institutional than relational, the husband/wife role is viewed as one of many. The husband/wife role is more important than some other roles such as volunteer, uncle/aunt, or brother/sister, but it often is too easily supplanted by other roles such as employee, parent, son/daughter, or friend. In a relational marriage the husband/wife role is established as priority. From that fixed position a couple can easily and quickly shift into another role as priority due to need, such as the birth of a baby, the acceptance of a new job, or a family crisis. This can be done because the couple can accept a temporary situation from a fixed position.

A second observation can be made. Where do individuals find the resources that make possible the continuing fulfillment of these roles that are vital to each of them? One of the best resources is in the creative power of the marital relationship. A good, healthy, growing marriage is energizing. To the contrary, a stagnant, dysfunctional marriage is de-energizing. When a couple establishes the husband/wife relationship as priority, the marital relationship accommodates the shifting into other roles based on need. The marital relationship nurtures and renews each partner, so there is energy to meet the demands of other valid and significant roles.

A Functional People

The American culture is one that is deeply rooted in functional living. In an early agrarian setting, later in an industrial setting, and presently in a high-tech one, functions are understood as primary, and relationships are secondary. The American dream that expresses itself in the rugged individualist who conquers and wins by hard work is functional by nature. Since life on a national level has been and still is motivated primarily by a sense of duty, the same is true in a historical understanding of marriage. David and Vera Mace wrote that it was not until the late 1930s or early 1940s that a new style of marriage, a companionship style, began to emerge as a possibility with real potential.[3] Couples since the forties have demonstrated a growing need and interest in a style of marriage in which functions, duties, prescribed roles, and adherence to established marital law are no longer dominant. The need and desire for an alternative style of marriage in which the relationship was primary, and the institutional needs and desires secondary, was forming and growing. An understanding of marriage was evolving in which grace, intimacy, shared meaning, and mutual love and support were established as the essence; works, functions, duties, roles, and rules were viewed as natural expressions of that grace. The familiar phrase, "Love and marriage go together like a horse and carriage" expresses the need to develop a new style of marriage. Thus, marriage, like the Christian experience, would be firmly established in a relationship where grace produced works rather than works producing grace. A relational style of marriage was born out of a need for companionship and continues to live and feed on that need.

The need for companionship, always present but now more clearly understood and identified, has remained fixed as an essential in marriage. The skills necessary for a couple to produce a growing relational marriage—a companionship one—are the primary focus of books, seminars, courses, and enrichment events. Marital skills are being treated as requirements, not electives. Couples' interest in what makes a marriage work, so they can be happy and stay away from serious marital problems and divorce, is causing them to be more cautious about marriage, to seek out serious premarital counseling, and to respond to opportunities to learn how to grow a strong, stable marriage. The interest is growing, but the use of such marital skills is still novel and untested by most couples.

Our educational system, both secular and religious, has taught us how to get a job, how to do a job, and how to keep a job. Neither has assumed serious responsibility for teaching us how to be prepared for marriage, how to establish a marriage, or how to build and keep a good marriage. For example, in all of my nineteen years of formal education, twelve in public schools, four at a private denominational institution, and three at a theological seminary, I had no courses that addressed a history of marriage or taught the skills that are needed to build a relational marriage. Because of my own inadequate preparation for a relational marriage, I later followed a new "call" to counsel with couples facing and experiencing marital stress. I began offering opportunities for couples to enrich their marriages—to make their good marriages better.

In any situation, marriage being no exception, an institution is not personal by nature. Its primary purpose is to identify and to accomplish its reasons for existence: to fulfill its goals by implementing the various functions and duties that are required to meet those goals. An institution can be personal by virtue of the persons who work within it.

Most couples today approach marriage with an expectation and intention to have a relational marriage. Their courtships have been relational, and they assume that their marriages will be the same. However, once married, many couples either quickly or slowly neglect the relational needs of the marriage. They establish a highly structural, effective functional marriage that runs and works well but in time loses its zest and vitality. There are reasons for this, and those reasons can be known and confronted. Thus, a marriage that expects and intends to be relational and begins that way can stay relational. These reasons will be closely identified and examined.

Jim and Linda have been married for ten years. They have the outward appearance of a solid marriage: they have three children; she is a homemaker; and he is a successful businessman. They are moderately active in their church and socially active in their community. Linda was the first to publicly acknowledge that her marriage was in a state of crisis. She sought treatment from her medical doctor for both depression and anxiety, and later she called the church office for an individual counseling appointment. Linda had sought to get Jim to join her, but Jim initially refused. After four sessions in which it was obvious that Linda's personal and emotional problems were directly related to the instability of the marriage, Jim agreed to come. In the first hour of conjoint counseling, having attained some valid marital history from the individual sessions, I shared with them the following marital design:

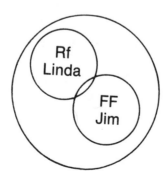

Then I offered the following diagnosis: Linda is primarily relational and secondarily functional in need, and Jim is excessively functional in need. Linda is fighting for a relationship in which she can continue to grow as a person and as a partner. Jim is fighting the business world. His fear of failure and his single-mindedness in pursuing success define for him personhood and partnership. Linda has become a crusader for a marital relationship and has been defeated, thus the depression and anxiety. Jim has held her off thus far with the benefits of business success. Their marriage is in a crisis for Linda personally and for the two of them maritally.

Notes

1. Robert Winch, *The Modern Family* (New York: Holt, 1963).
2. Dr. David Mace, *We Can Have Better Marriages.*
3. Ibid.

2

Relational/Functional Combinations

Marriage is a relationship between two persons in which the "coupleness" in the marriage is a creation that reflects the individuality of the two partners plus the unique combinations that occur when the individualities are mixed. It can be illustrated this way:

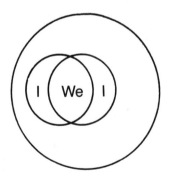

One of the marked traits that persons bring to marriage is whether they tend to be more functional or relational in need. By functional I mean a person who has been developmentally designed primarily to perform some operation, duty, job, or task. A functional person is product directed, goal and work oriented, and likes for roles to be clearly defined and assigned. A relational person is one who has been developmentally designed to see and to seek relationships as the core to a healthy, full life. A person who is relational is person oriented, process directed, and open to shared roles.

In marriage, since differences attract, it is not uncommon for persons with strong functional needs to be attracted to persons with strong relational needs. This difference that attracts is also one of the primary sources of conflict in the marriage. Each person brings to marriage his or her own personal orientation, and the marriage is given the task of integrating those differing orientations creatively, constructively, and productively. Following are five marriages that reflect the relational/functional differences, the combinations that are present in each marriage, the marital dynamics, and the results. In the diagrams the F is functional, the R is relational, the FR is functional/relational, and the RF is relational/functional. The combinations note the mixtures.

1. Functional/Relational

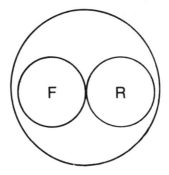

Joe and Jill met in college. They had a long-term courtship and got married while he was in graduate school. Now they have three children. Joe is a successful lawyer, and Jill is a homemaker. The marital status is one of crisis. Joe grew up in a family where he learned early that by achievement he could escape the confinement and the embarrassment of his family. He made it with his peers by being both a jock and a scholar. He continued this obsessive pursuit through college, graduate school, and into his law practice. Jill's family expected her to achieve in high school and in college, but the stronger, often unspoken program for her was marriage, family, and homemaking. A college education was valid for her primarily for personal growth, exposure, and for external security so that if necessary, either because of economics or emergency, she would be more marketable in the job world. Jill came into the marriage with high expectations, nurtured by her family and out of her own needs. Joe entered into marriage determined to provide for his family all that he had missed out on as a child and adolescent in his own family. Work was the way to do it. He became a successful lawyer who amply took care of the basic physical needs of his family, but he became to them the present stranger. Jill's requests for companionship were rejected; and, in reaction to the constant rejection, the requests soon felt like demands to Joe. In reaction to her demands, he used anger and conflict to justify his need to give more and more time to his work. In exchange for himself, Joe showered Jill with surprises—flowers, perfume, candies, and trips—all perceived by her as "cheap grace." As she said, "He tried to buy me off so he could go on as is and even have my support." She was seen by him as a demanding wife, and he was seen by her as a calloused, insensitive, and selfish husband.

2. Relational-Relational

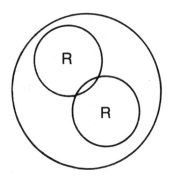

Beth and Bob grew up in contrasting styles of families, but both entered into marriage with a high level of relational needs. Bob was an only child who grew up with loving and accepting parents. His family always took time to listen to his feelings and opinions, and they encouraged his participation. Bob's parents expected him to perform certain tasks, functions, and responsibilities in the family; but if he failed to accomplish one of his assigned chores, no big deal was made out of it. The needs of the house or the yard or the church could be set aside for the needs of the family to go and do things together. As a child, Bob had friends, and as an adolescent he was liked and accepted by his peers. School was important, but friends were more important.

Beth grew up in a family in which she was the middle child. An older brother and a younger sister, as often is the case, squeezed Beth from both sides so that her emotional needs were overlooked or ignored. Even though the family was stable and dependable, Beth felt the "squeeze" as a child and often had feelings of being left out or left behind. The stability of the family compensated for some of her feelings, and that enabled her to leave childhood and move through adolescence with a rather clear understanding of where she was and what had happened. She was aware of her need for someone who would see her and relate to her as a special person. Beth was aware of the need but not aware of its intensity.

In college Beth and Bob met and were quickly attracted to each other. Their relational needs were highly complimentary. Abundance and scarcity had created for this couple a complimentary high level of need for emotional attention and support. While attending a marriage enrichment event, they were able to affirm their marriage for addressing their emotional needs for companionship. They also were able to identify more clearly the primary source of unresolved conflict that had begun to seriously effect their marriage. Vocational identity, financial, household, and parenting responsibilities—the functional needs of the marriage—were of much less importance to Bob than to Beth. Beth was expected to carry the functional aspect of the marriage, and it created a new situation for her. As a child in her family she felt safe and secure. Now she felt insecure. A growing fear and anger developed in Beth that she sought to ignore and suppress. Eventually, she became depressed, and the expression of their relational needs was blocked. The depression was the impetus for seeking marital counseling.

3. Functional/Functional

Tom and Doris met in graduate school. Both were ambitious students who were highly motivated by their desire to find good jobs where they could achieve and succeed. Neither was interested in having a serious relationship. They enjoyed each other's company and talked openly about their academic pursuits and their professional goals. Both landed jobs in the same city, and they continued to see each other. Both were in their late twenties. External and internal expectations to marry and start a

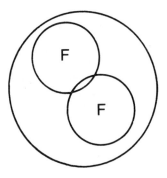

family worked on both of them. Their higher need for professional achievement and stability was complimentary. Their lower needs for relational living and the fulfillment of their own and other's expectations combined to support a strong case for marriage.

Tom, an only child, grew up in a single-parent family where he was put in a position to resolve the agenda created by his parents' divorce. In some sense, his mother expected him to be what his father was not. He was to be the success that would eliminate, or at least minimize, the failure of the marriage. In order not to be seen as a mother's boy, Tom felt he had to be a bodybuilder and a sports enthusiast. To be somebody, he needed to be highly independent, physically strong and attractive, and professionally successful. Marriage was a possibility if he could find a partner who, in wanting the same things, would support his need to be primarily functional and secondarily relational.

Doris appeared to be that perfect partner. She grew up in a very relational family. Her parents were professionally established and successful, and within her family the importance of vocational identity and achievement were highly regarded. The five children were exposed to the importance of both relational living and vocational success. Doris, through her childhood and adolescence, developed a growing suspicion regarding marriage and began to establish and pursue as a priority a professional career to deal with those feelings of uncertainty and suspicion. She took pride in her established position and frequently stated publicly that marriage was not for her. Underneath that highly developed professional cover was a tenderness that related to her need for family and relational living.

Tom and Doris were married for three years, and they avidly pursued their professional goals. They sought to support each other in their individual pursuits, and the functional marriage worked well. Slowly, the relational needs buried deeply and securely under Doris's professional cover peeped out, then crept out, and, finally, stood out. Her relational needs, suppressed under a refined functional marriage, created a wedge between them, eventually brought them to marriage counseling, and ultimately to divorce.

4. Functional-Relational/Relational-Functional

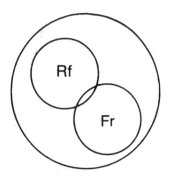

Carl and Kathy have been married for twenty years. They have two teenagers. The primary issue in their marital relationship has been that of affection. Carl grew up in a rural setting on a farm in a large, patriarchal family. His father's strong, authoritative manner, together with his provisional love for his son, caused Carl to believe he could not be strong *and* tender. Carl's mother was loving, but maternal duties kept her so busy that usually she expressed affection only when someone was hurt or sick. Affirmation, when either parent gave it, was usually after a function completed and well done.

Kathy was the first of three children. She and her family lived in a moderately sized city where her family was known. As a child she received lots of affection from both parents, but especially so from her father. Even now when she and her father visit, they still sit and hold hands. Kathy was a very obedient, functional child and adolescent, but her obedience and functioning were an expression of her paternal acceptance and love, not a way to get it.

Kathy and Carl met, dated, and got married. Several years into the marriage they became aware that there was conflict. It would come and go but never stay away. They attended a marriage-enrichment event at church where they were introduced to the concept that although differences attract, differences are also one of the primary sources of marital conflict. Carl was like Kathy's father in that he was functionally strong and dependable, but he was unlike him in that he did not express a need for, or give, much affection. Carl was functionally relational, Kathy was relationally functional, and the marital conflict grew out of the difference.

5. Relational-Functional/Relational-Functional

Becky and David have been married for twelve years. In their marriage they have worked to keep their relationship first, special, and growing. David and Becky came from very similar backgrounds. They both grew up in small towns where their homes were open places to each one in the family and to their friends. Family was a

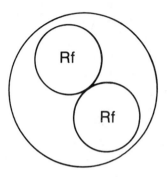

high priority, and the marriage relationship primary in the family. Both knew that their parents were special to each other and that their parents' marriages were stable, warm, loving, and open. What they saw modeled was good, and they learned from their models what was important and how to build and grow a good marriage. Functions were important but never as important as each other and their relationship. What David and Becky had seen and experienced as children they now were working out in their own marriage. They knew how to express their needs, how to deal with and resolve conflict, how to make roles subservient to personal needs, and how to be creative and spontaneous as lovers. Their marriage was not perfect, but it was working and growing.

Summary

The five marital styles produced by the varying combinations of functional/relational needs create observable marital patterns that produce some predictable results.

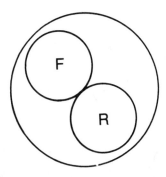

The functional/relational style of marriage has a high divorce rate. Marital therapy is long-term. Therapy has to work with established patterns and personality change.

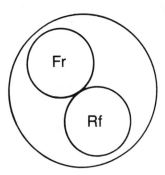

The functional-relational/relational-functional have all the common elements necessary for a good marriage and often respond well to counseling as they are helped to mediate and integrate their differences. These couples participate well in marriage enrichment events.

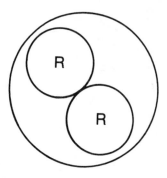

The relational/relational style is often seen in the pre-marital stage or in the first years of marriage. Love is all-important, and the growing responsibilities that are indigenous to marriage and family are not accepted or handled well. Thus the growing marital stress and tension will become a wedge that separates or a bridge over which they walk to build a more realistic, appropriately functional marriage.

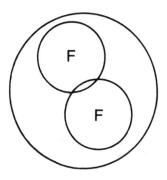

The functional/functional marriage is sturdy and dry. If the two partners, due to their backgrounds and needs, remain functional, they can build a life together, but it is centered around goals and duties—the by-products of marriage are primary. If either one makes a move toward the other to involve him or her in a more relational way, the marriage is threatened. Either the move is denied, or the persistence of the one making the move will cause such conflict that the marriage will dissolve and separate. The one who opts for change will often seek counseling, but the other will stubbornly refuse to participate.

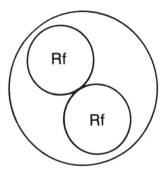

The relational-functional/relational-functional couples seldom seek counseling, but they are the couples most responsive to the invitation to participate in marital growth experiences such as marriage enrichment events, seminars, and church or community events related to marriage and the family.

3

Initial Hour

Marriage is a friendship that grows as it changes and changes as it grows.

The initial hour with a marriage counselor—either a highly trained marriage and family therapist or a skilled listener, such as a pastor—is critical. The initial hour is critical if it is marital therapy or if it is marriage enrichment. Couples who come, whether to get help and relief from a crisis or to get enriched, bring their resistance. In marriage-enrichment events, partners are jokingly referred to as "draggers" and "dragees."

The initial session in marital growth and enrichment is critical for several reasons. First, clients or participants have to be "hooked" in the first session so that the counseling relationship will get the time and build the trust necessary to work on the issues that cause the marital stress. In marriage enrichment, the first session is critical because couples need to see quickly that all marriages have growth areas and room for enrichment.

A second reason the initial hour is so important is that couples expect from the first session of therapy, or enrichment, what they expect from their medical doctor. They expect, on their first visit, both a diagnosis and a prognosis. The best way for a doctor to lose a potential patient or a patient is to act overconfident, underconfident, confused, or uncertain about his role in the doctor-patient relationship. If the doctor is uncertain, he claims that uncertainty, and he can either indicate the need for more testing or refer to another doctor who is a specialist in the area that seems appropriate for the manifested symptoms. On their first visit to their doctor, patients want and need to know what is wrong and what needs to be done.

The same is true for couples who seek marital counseling or growth. They want to know what is going on and what can be done about it. Counselors can address this need in many ways during the initial hour or session. With couples who seek marital counseling, I employ different images to defuse the feelings of frustration and out-of-controlledness. Three such images are a cat and a ball of yarn, a wall built by unresolved conflict, and circles within a circle that depict a functional, relational marriage. The first is verbal, and the other two are visual.

A couple in the midst of a dysfunctional marriage feels very much like you might feel when you walk into a room where a cat has had the uninterrupted pleasure of playing with a ball of yarn. The yarn is everywhere, tangled, and knotted. The situation offers several choices. You can scold the cat, but that does not address or affect the state of the yarn. The easiest thing to do is to pick up the yarn, throw it away, and either give up the project for which the yarn was intended, or go and buy a new spool of yarn. In a sense, the same options are present for the couple. They can scold each other, and the marriage will grow worse. They can gather it together and throw it away, making possible the prospect of another one. They can take the time and make the effort to find the beginning place, unknot and unravel the yarn, and then use the yarn for what it was intended: a meaningful relationship.

A second image to use in the initial hour that gives both a diagnosis and a prognosis is a visual one. I draw for the couple the following figures:

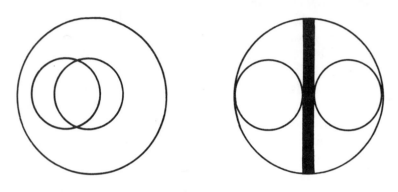

Fig. 1   **Fig. 2.**

Couples who are unhappy with their marriages and seek marital counseling usually are upset and angry with each other. The anger usually is not produced by any one marital issue such as sex, finances, in-laws, children, or friends, but by several or many. The unresolved conflict produced by one or all of these issues brought them to counseling. In figure one, the marital relationship is working well. In figure two, the couple is still legally married, but the relationship is separated, divorced by a wall of unresolved conflict produced by unmet needs. The villain is the wall that must be taken down brick by brick rather than by a demolition ball, as initially preferred and tried by many couples.

The third image (see p. 45, top) can be used as a diagnostic tool in the initial hour for either marital counseling or enrichment. It is the functional/relational dynamic present to varying degrees in each marriage.

The couple(s) is handed a sheet of paper on which is printed the five distinguishing characteristics between a relational marriage and a functional marriage. Those marital characteristics provide the counselor/couple, enrichment leader/couples, a broad but thorough entree into the problem and growth areas of their marriage(s).

A growth area in marriage is like a tiny pebble in your shoe. You can keep walking, but the irritation is constant. If you address the issue—remove the pebble—you can walk with more comfort and ease. The same is not true with a stone. You can shift the stone to the edge, but it will return. The stone will cause so much discomfort and pain that the only way to continue is to stop, take off the shoe, remove the stone, put back on the shoe, and continue to walk. In marriage, the pebble is a growth area. If it is not addressed, it will grow into a stone. A stone is a marital problem.

These characteristics that are present in a marriage can be pebbles or stones. If pebbles, they respond well to marriage enrichment. If they are stones, they require marital counseling.

1. Change Versus Sameness

   A relational marriage is characterized by flexibility, adventure, spontaneity, and creativity. A functional marriage is more predictable, rigid, boring, and routine.

2. Communication: Feelings Versus Facts

   In a relational marriage, feelings are as valid as facts and are easily and continually shared. Communication in a functional marriage is heavily factual.

3. Conflict Resolution Versus Unresolved Conflict.

   A relational marriage requires conflict resolution while a functional marriage is often supported by unresolved conflict.

4. Intimacy Versus Sex

In a relational marriage, sex is not enough. Sex is one of the many expressions of intimacy. In functional marriages, sex is enough. It is physical and devoid of intimacy.

5. Emotional Needs Versus Physical Needs.

In a relational marriage, emotional needs are treated as valid as physical needs, while a functional marriage centers around physical needs, food, clothing, and shelter.

Each of these differences will be carefully and fully considered in the next section of the book. Each chapter includes an exercise form at the end for you to use in evaluating your marriage. Through the exercises, you will learn how relational or functional you perceive your marriage to be using each of the five distinguishing characteristics. At the end of the chapter on emotional needs versus physical needs, the form will be completed, and each of you will have an overall view of how the other views your marriage. Then you can use the evaluations to talk about where you are maritally.

The exercise can be helpful in several ways.

1. It reveals marital perceptions. A person's behavior is a response to either perceived reality or reality. Through the exercise each partner is made aware of the other's perceptions about the state of the marriage.

2. The exercise reveals the temperature of the marriage in that the assigned score can be measured over against the potential score.

3. The exercise tags more specific marital growth areas or reveals potential marital problem areas.

4. A couple's score can be measured over against collected data from other couples who have participated in the exercise, either as couples in counseling or as couples in marriage enrichment. (Check the statistical data at the conclusion of the book.)

4

Change Versus Sameness

*Marriage is a friendship that grows as it changes
and changes as it grows.*

Anything that is alive changes. Only dead things remain the same. Marriage is an alive relationship. Thus, change is as essential to marriage as love, and change is one of love's most cordial friends. To the contrary, common enemies of marriage that test marriage early in its existence are boredom and sameness. Routine creates predictability, and predictability nurtures boredom and sameness.

One of the most exciting aspects of the courting relationship is spontaneity. When the courting stays alive in marriage and feeds the relationship, two people enjoy each other. There is adventure in their relationship. They discover each other through both the known and the openness to the yet to be tried, sought, and discovered. As the relationship grows into a form that is more predictable and permanent, it also remains open. It is open to the excitement that is always present to two persons who want to discover the internal nature of each other and their relationship and the external nature of their common world composed of people, places, things, and events.

It is a sad commentary on marriage when people say of two persons in a courting relationship, "They are beginning to act like married folks." Such a comment means the excitement and fun of a courting relationship is giving way to the settledness and predictability of married folks who often feel bound, boxed in, and bored. A relational marriage is one that blends the adventure of courting with the structure and stability of marriage. The functional marriage is one that slowly gives up the excitement of courting for the structure and predictability of marriage.

One of the benefits that I now enjoy as an adult, but which I disliked as a child and adolescent, is having grown up on a farm. As an adolescent and young adult, I sought to structure my life so no one would know I was a farm boy. I thought I had arrived when a close college friend told me that he never knew I was a country boy. As an adult, I seldom enter into a new relationship, whether it be a new friend or a counselee, that my "farm boy self" does not make itself evident. So much of who I am, how I think and see things, comes from my childhood and adolescent years on the farm.

I remember as a child on the farm in south Alabama that access roads to the various parcels of land making up our farm were two deeply cut ruts. Those ruts ran through the sandy bottoms and over the rolling clay hills. If we wanted to get to the field, or the pond, or the shelter, then we had to follow the ruts. But to stay in the ruts was to see only parts of the farm. In those places where the ground was firm or where grass was planted, we could leave the ruts. We could find a way to the places where the deer grazed or the new calf was born, or we could find a place where we could drink the clear, cool water from the bubbling spring. All of the farm was available to us, but we had to leave the old ruts and frequently cut some new paths to get where we wanted and needed to go.

In marriage, couples either by neglect or by choice travel only in the ruts. Thus, they seldom experience or discover the inherent potential that is present in every marriage. Marriage certainly needs the ruts, but if a couple settles for a marital relationship accessible only by the ruts of sameness and predictability, they have chosen to forego the relational joy that goes with creative growth and change. They have chosen to be functionally married rather than relationally married.

A friend of ours told us how she had nurtured the courting aspect of her growing marriage with the following plan. On Thursday evening, without her husband's knowledge, she consulted with their children about her weekend plan. She made the necessary arrangements, packed their clothes, and went to bed bubbling with the excitement of her secret. As was their daily custom, they drove to work together the following morning. The wife dropped her husband off at his work, clocked in for a half-day at work, and returned home to finish some last minute responsibilities. Later she picked up her husband on schedule and asked if he had any errands to run. (He is known for his errands after work!) After driving him to several places, getting all errands completed, she asked, "Are you ready to go?" "Yes," he replied and settled back to relax. Aware that they were not going home, he waited curiously for an explanation. When he got none, he finally said, "I take it that we are not going home." "You are right," she replied and kept driving. After driving south for an hour, they arrived in a resort community. She had made reservations for the weekend in one of the mountain motels, rated high by its honeymooners who need only a place to share their budding romance and by "ole" married folks who need a place and time to renew their courtship and romance.

Another couple whose marriage was struggling to stay

alive went on periodic rendezvous, but with different results. Mike is a young man who is married to his need to succeed. This need expressed itself in the relentless drive to sell and to move up the corporate ladder. He is sensitive to the rights of marriage and his children, but they are rationalized away and sacrificed to his need to achieve. The drive is maintained and fed both by his developmental feelings of inadequacy and his family background, in which persons were valued in terms of production and success. The benefit of his insatiable drive to succeed—an advancing income—provides for his wife and children a style of living that he considers a valid substitute for his lack of presence. The children are small and limited in the way they express their disapproval of how their father substitutes things for himself. His wife, Jan, verbalized her complaint, then argued her case, acted it out with sexual frigidity, developed physical symptoms from the mounting stress and frustration, and, after finally threatening divorce without results, sought personal counseling.

One of Jan's primary sources of anger toward Mike was the way he sought to buy her off. Periodically he came home and would announce or invite Jan on a week-long or weekend trip—a trip either earned from his zealous sales or from his need to rest. Needing a break from her continuous parenting role and responsibility, Jan would respond affirmatively to Mike's invitation. The plan usually failed. Mike saw the trip as compensation for his lack of marital time and interest, and Jan saw it as a time to rest and relax from her "single" parent role. Mike wanted to honeymoon, and Jan wanted to find a haven in which to hibernate from the constant care of their children. The trips became less and less frequent as they failed to accomplish their task. Instead of marital renewal and refreshment, the marriage experienced more disappointment and greater estrangement.

In a functional marriage, even times of renewal and enrichment are predictable. They usually are calendared, or they occur according to finances, or they are the byproduct of some other family, church, or community event. A relational marriage plans events that feed the marriage, but it is also nurtured by the more spontaneous momentary experiences that grow out of the creative will.

In the dating relationship, we refer to the creative will as romance. Romance is very much like the wind. It has a will to do and to accomplish, but it is also free to move and dance at will. The presence of romance is one of the differences between a marriage that is predictable and arid and one that stays alive to the beat of surprise and innovation.

Romance is defined as the way marriage partners keep alive the knowledge and feelings of being special to each other. A person who grows up in a family feeling special as a child expects that in marriage. When it is present in courtship and continues into early marriage and then ebbs and disappears, the partner often feels rejected or taken for granted. For persons who have not experienced being special to someone, there is the need for it; and that need, if not met, can become almost insatiable. To be special to each other in marriage does not appear to be that important until it is not present. It is like perfume. It is not needed to abundance, but a touch of it adds a flavor that creatively enhances the marriage.

Romance ceases to be romance in a marriage if it is limited to special dates and occasions like birthdays and Christmas. All the special days and occasions are built-in opportunities to be thoughtful and kind and to make each other feel special. If couples use only those times, the special gives way to the predictable. Special days are kept special by the other days when marital partners are creative and spontaneous in communicating to the other how neat and special he/she is. Romance needs the calendar, but it ceases to be romance if it is limited to the calendar.

I keep a file at my office entitled "Personal Keepsakes." To illustrate the freedom of "specialness" to use both calendared dates and creative moments, I opened that folder, and here are some of the expressions I found:

"Dad, just wanted to say I hope you have a great day, and you're in my heart especially today! (Couple of others are too!) Hope this valentine is a special one for you! Love ya, Meredith."

A note from my son, Bob, concluded with these words, "You are a great dad and a special friend."

My wife is a "card wife." She does not just buy a card. She buys *the* card. Occasionally, and just frequently enough, I find a card from her mailed to me at the office. The ones for calendared days I get at home, hand delivered. The unexpected ones I get on other days are mailed: "Something special just to show you . . .
. . . it's something special just to know you" (Hallmark).

On a particular card, a small sad, blue bird sits painfully alone and thinks:
"Without you . . .
(inside) . . . nothin' swings!"

My wife added, "I'm glad we're swinging!"

When our third child was several months old, my wife took Jeff to visit her parents in South Carolina. She needed the rest and affirmation she always receives when she visits her home. After that visit I received from her the following letter:

"Hello, love. I always did like love letters . . . hope you still do!

"The roses went out today, but the fragrance remains. Thank you for the lovely thought and also for the perfect single one in Jeff's room. I know he is going to bring us joy in all the years ahead . . . I feel it in my heart.

"Thank you for enabling me to go home with confidence and at ease about how you three would be here. I appreciate all you did for Bob and Meredith and hope the days had special hours for you as father with the children. My visit was one I needed, and the timing was so right for Mother and Daddy.

"I especially want you to know how loved you have made me feel during these days. Thank you for the superlatives you have been free to give . . . words like *wonderful* and even that new one, "marvelous." For whatever reason, to be told one is marvelous is a thrilling and powerful thing. I love you with all that I am, and I love you for loving me. Always, Sydnor."

My file of personal keepsakes is added to more frequently than my wife's, but we both are aware of the marital benefit we receive from our "personal keepsakes." A relational marriage is one in which romance is kept alive and loving while a functional marriage is one in which romance is snuffed out, either quickly or slowly, by choosing to live only in the ruts.

From a Christian perspective, romance could be understood to be the presence of grace in the midst of works. If romance is primarily understood as keeping the feelings of being special present in the marital relationship, then from a Christian perspective we can call that grace. Grace is our being special to God because of who we are. It cannot be earned or limited to special days or events. One of the rare qualities of biblical grace is its spontaneity.

Grace from God is both a state and an expression. It is not enough to know that I live in grace. I need the reassurance and joy of grace daily. Grace is who God is, and it is also what God does. I do not have to earn His love. That is given. I do need to experience His love so that I am graced daily by that love. Grace is not only of God for us, but it is of me to you and you to me.

Grace in marriage is that state of being special so that I do not have to earn it. Also, grace is a creative love that finds innumerable ways to keep alive and current those feelings of being special.

One of the clearest and richest insights we have into the person of Jesus is John's vivid account of the triangular drama involving the scribes and the Pharisees, an adulterous woman, and Jesus (John 7:53—8:11). The dynamics of the drama are tense and alive, the struggle for truth powerful, and the value of persons as understood from two opposing systems highly conflictual. The drama is told not to reveal one truth but many truths. The one truth for this moment is that in the scribes' and Pharisees' system of works there was no place for the expression of grace. Not only was their system fixed and determined, it was functional and predictable. In their system the woman was no longer special, just judged and condemned. The system was to be maintained at the expense of a person.

Into that sterile system Jesus brought redemptive grace. In His presence the judgment on her, as prescribed by the law, slowly dissipated. The presence of grace identified and restored her sense of being special. She was related to as a person of infinite value.

Jesus never claimed at any point the demise of the law. He said, on one occasion, that it was not His purpose to destroy the law but to fulfill it (Matt. 5:17). Law was and is necessary. To keep law from being sterile, harsh, and fixed, it needs the fragrance of grace.

So does marriage. Grace in marriage is both a state and an expression. It is the knowledge that our specialness is not earned but given. It is the creative ways that love expresses specialness. In a functional marriage, works are a high priority. In a relational marriage, grace punctuates the works with a creativity and spontaneity that cause each partner to feel special to the other.

Another aspect of a relational marriage as over against a functional one is that of growth. The Christian life is analogous at this point. Paul, writing to the Christians as Ephesus, noted the necessity for growth and provided a measurable model when he wrote: "We are not meant to remain as children at the mercy of every chance wind of teaching, and of the jockeying of men who are expert in the crafty presentation of lies. But we are meant to speak the truth in love, and to grow up in every way into Christ, the head" (Eph. 4:14-15, Phillips).

Every healthy relationship is one that grows and changes. A relationship cannot stay the same. It either grows and matures, or it atrophies and dies. The marriage relationship is no exception.

The beginning of marriage can be compared to a new baby. All the potential for adulthood is there but not yet realized. Growth is the road over which an infant walks from childhood to adulthood. In marriage, two mature adults make a commitment to each other, but they still create a new relationship that is infantile in its beginning. The maturity of the two committing adults affects significantly that new potential infant, but the newness of that relationship is still novel. Each marriage is unique and different in that it has the personal flavor of the two individuals. All marriages are alike in that the relationship in its initial stage is new and untried. The growth pattern of each marriage is both peculiarly individualistic and commonly predictable. In a relational marriage growth is experienced in terms of some peaks and valleys, but it is moving and changing. The relationship changes and grows as the partners share and learn about each other. Each partner sees the other as an inexhaustible resource that is known yet unknown. Each new insight gathered, each new fact discovered, and each new experience shared is channeled through the relationship, nurturing change and growth in the marriage.

As to growth, several possibilities are indigenous to each marriage: (1) one partner may grow and leave the other; (2) Both partners may see growth as essential to personal and marital health, and support each other in that individual development; (3) The couple may focus almost totally on the functional aspects of the marriage, in which case growth is measured primarily in terms of the status of the marital institution, not the marital relationship. If the third option is true, marital duties are high priorities and are performed well. The institution appears to be working well, but the inner core, the relationship, is malnourished and ignored. Sooner or later the marriage becomes a solid shell with a hollow core. If two people want no more, it stands. Today that is becoming more rare. As Dr. David M. Mace has clearly said, "If marriages stay together today, it is due primarily to internal cohesion, not external coercion."[1] A marriage that is committed to growth and change is a relational marriage. A marriage that is comfortable with established duties and rules, sameness, is a functional marriage.

Relational/Functional Exercise

Using the five-noted characteristics contrasting a relational and functional marriage, each marriage partner is to evaluate his or her marriage as relational or functional. The scale is one to ten, ten being the maximum relational. Give first your own perception of how you see the marriage and then give your perception of how your partner sees the marriage.

Functional   Relational

---

1   2   3   4   5   6   7   8   9   10

h   w

1. Change versus sameness

Flexibility vs. Rigidity

1. Make a list of ten ways you like to be shown that you are special to your spouse. Make the list and then ask your mate to prioritize them as he/she perceives them to be important to you. An example follows.

When you have completed the exercise, talk about it with your mate. Pay attention to what you already knew, what surprised you about your partner, and what you learned to be important.

Husband's list   Wife's perception
  1. Verbal "I love you"
  2. Sexual initiative
  3. Well-chosen card
  4. Personal note or letter
  5. Interest in my daily life
  6. Massage
  7. Evening out
  8. Unexpected phone call

9. Courting and appreciating in
public
10. Time away from family

Wife's list   Husband's perception
 1. Verbal "I love you"
 2. Unexpected phone call
 3. Well-chosen card
 4. Time away from family
 5. Sexual initiative
 6. Personal note or letter
 7. Evening out
 8. Massage
 9. Courting and appreciating in
public
10. Interest in my daily life

2. Times My Husband/Wife Made Me Feel Special
   Write in twenty-five words or less something your partner did for you in the past that made you feel very special to him or her.

Husband for Wife:
   In the past week: _____

_____
_____

   In the past year: _____

_____
_____

   Since we were married: _____

_____
_____

Wife for Husband:
   In the past week: _____

_____
_____

In the past year: _____

_____

_____

Since we were married: _____

_____

_____

3. Learning from Scripture: Gifts

The following passages of Scripture have as a focus an expression of grace: a surprise gift. Read them individually, and then talk about them as a couple. Use the following questions to guide your discussion:

1. Identify the area of surprise. What was expected and what actually occurred?

2. Identify the gift. What does the gift accomplish?

3. What gifts are present in each passage that we can give to each other?

Passage 1: Luke 15:11-24
Passage 2: Mark 10:46-52
Passage 3: Luke 7:36-50

4. Share an experience in which you were "graced" by the other and what it meant to you.

Notes

1. Dr. David Mace, *We Can Have Better Marriages.*

5

Communication: Feelings Versus Facts

Communication is the invitation we extend to each other to join the other on the exciting and risky journey of self-disclosure and self-discovery.

At its best, communication is defined in marriage as the invitation we extend to each other join each other on the exciting and risky journey of self-disclosure and self-discovery. The invitation is, at times, natural and easy. Frequently, it is intentional and difficult.

Whether communication in marriage is natural or intentional—and for all marriages it is some of both—it is essential. Both a functional marriage and a relational marriage depend on communication. In any relationship, functional or dysfunctional, open or closed, communication occurs. Communication is indigenous to a relationship. Communication can be effective or ineffective, verbal or nonverbal. It can be over or under, against or around. It takes many shapes and forms, but in every marriage it is present.

As a marriage counselor, I discovered that communication is the most frequently given response couples make to the question, "What is the nature of your problem?" Communication to marital relationships is very much like the common cold to health. If communication is not good in marriage, the total relationship "feels" bad.

There is so much biblical permission and support for

feelings and the expression of them. Even in one's relationship with God the whole gamut of feelings is openly present and acknowledged. One of the best collections of a person's expressed feelings as related to God is the Psalms. The psalmist is presented in a variety of settings in which various feelings are viewed as natural and appropriate.

In Psalm 8, the psalmist was reflecting on humankind, God, and the relationship of the two. He celebrated the very nature and character of God with joy and gladness as he proclaimed, "O Lord, our Lord, how majestic is thy name in all the earth!"

Over against the majesty of God, the psalmist reflected on human beings. Having a good day, the psalmist did not cower or retreat, but he stood appropriately proud and celebrated the glory of humanity by reflecting:

Yet thou hast made him little less than God,
and dost crown him with glory and honor.
Thou hast given him dominion over the works of thy hands; . . .

And even in between, the majesty of God on one hand and the honor of humankind on the other, the psalmist marveled at the creation and was glad in it.

When I look at thy heavens, the work of thy fingers,
the moon and the stars which thou hast established;
what is man that thou art mindful of him,
and the son of man that thou dost care for him?

The psalmist opened his life with a song and shared his joy found in God, in being, and in creation, and he sang it for all to hear. He felt glad, and he shared it.

For the psalmist, however, the mood was always changing. In Psalm 22 there is deep anguish and sadness, bordering on despair, because the psalmist feels abandoned. His friend and companion, so attentive, was now gone and did not return. The psalmist lifted the window of his life and cried out his sadness. He began with a shout and ended with a whisper:

> My God, my God, why hast thou forsaken me?
> Why art thou so far from helping me, from the words of my groaning?
> O my God, I cry by day, but thou dost not answer;
> and by night, but find no rest.

The psalmist was buried in his sadness, and he cried out to the world. He felt sad, and he shared it.

In Psalm 51, the psalmist examined himself and found himself wanting. In the presence of his sinful life and of God's strong and loving nature, he acknowledged and expressed his guilt. He was contrite (felt badly) and held it up to the world.

> O God, as thou art kind, have mercy upon me,
> in thy vast pity wipe out my offences,
> wash me from every stain of guilt,
> and purge me from my sin.
> Well do I know my offences;
> my sin is never out of mind.
> It is against thee I have sinned,
> I have done evil in thy sight (vv. 1-4, Moffatt).

The psalmist felt bad, and he shared it.

The psalmist was a different character in Psalm 137. Taken from his homeland into captivity where he was separated from familiar places and people, the psalmist vacillated between quitting and fighting. In his anger he knew what he wanted to do but could not. So he asked God to do for him what he was unable to accomplish.

> Remember, O Lord, against the Edomites
> the day of Jerusalem,
> how they said, "Raze it, raze it!
> Down to its foundations!"

> O daughter of Babylon, you devastator!
> Happy shall he be who requites you
> with what you have done to us!
> Happy shall he be who takes your little ones
> and dashes them against the rock!

It was obvious that the psalmist was mad, and he shared it.

The psalmist was one of the biblical models who felt mad, sad, glad, and bad, and he shared his feelings. The biblical model is clear: Feelings are not just for some of us; they belong to all of us. Feelings are not to be kept. They are to be shared appropriately.

Several general observations about communicating feelings appropriately can be made here. First, over the past couple of decades or so, the market has been flooded with books, pamphlets, seminars, films, etc., focusing on communication as an essential to good relationships. This focus has raised the marital consciousness to a much higher level about the importance of good communication in marriage. At the same time, it also has created a handy, available catchall in which many couples deposit all sorts of marital problems. Second, new and better communication skills are needed in marriages whether a couple is facing a marital crisis or engaging in marital enrichment. Third, and more specific to our purpose, how a couple communicates serves as a visible clue to whether their marriage is functional or relational. Functional marriages communicate primarily, sometimes almost totally, with facts. In a relational marriage, feelings as well as facts are valued and expressed.

A historical review of marriage reveals that marriage as an institution was highly influenced by other related institutions like the public school, the factory, and the church. In these places, duties and functions were primary and relationships secondary. A person's value was determined by hard work and achievement. Communication was factual and objective with little room for feelings. Information, facts, and decisions based on objective truth were sought and underscored. Subjective truth that reflected feelings and interpretations did not fit well into the developing scientific and industrial complex that viewed truth as factual—that which could be observed, measured, and used. The church was a friendly companion to this developing industrial complex in that it took the Old Testament family model, the patriarchal one, in which the man was dominant and roles and functions were clearly defined and observed. In this family model, just as in the school and the factory, feelings were seldom expressed and were usually controlled.

Historically, men have been cast in the family role of provider, and this has had lasting effects. Women have been primarily responsible for the building and sustaining of the relationships in the family. In their respective roles, men were expected to communicate in the family factually and rationally. Feelings were minimized, ignored, or suppressed. This was epitomized in the often-heard advice to boys, "Big boys don't cry." Women and girls were understood to be "feelers" and "criers." As a result, they often were described as overly sensitive, fragile, moody, unpredictable, and dependent. In contrast, men were seen as strong and independent. While women were programmed to be relational, men were taught to be functional. In the marriage of the two, women wanted and needed to talk about feelings, and men restricted their communication primarily to facts. What worked in the job seemed to leave much lacking in the marriage.

The wife had feelings: she was comfortable with them,

and she wanted to share them both for personal and marital reasons. The husband, who was uncomfortable talking about his own feelings, was not responsive to another who wanted to share with him her feelings. Usually a person who does not value the need to talk about feelings does not value the need to listen to feelings. Historically, the marital relationship that brings together one partner who is programmed to be relational and another who is programmed to be functional begins with a communication handicap. To one, feelings are valued and to be shared. To the other, feelings are invalid and to be suppressed.

These learned communication tendencies and skills are present to varying degrees in every marriage. In evaluating a marriage, whether the evaluation is done personally or professionally, a marriage in which the couple shares feelings freely and frequently is usually a marriage that is relational in character and expression. On the other hand, a marriage that communicates factually and rationally is a functional one. In counseling, when a couple expresses opinions on the state of their marriage, ineffective communication is identified frequently as the critical problem. What the husband usually means by this is that he and his wife are not able to sit down, talk things out, and come to some workable conclusion or solution. The wife usually means that she and her husband do not talk about their feelings; thus, he does not know her, and she does not know him.

In saying that relational marriages communicate feelings as well as facts and that functional marriages tend to talk facts and leave feelings unspoken, I appeal to one of the basic tenets of polemics: exaggeration. The exaggeration is present here to make the point, but it does not alter the truth.

Mack and Jan are a couple who brought an enormous

amount of their past into their marriage. They were having a difficult time correcting an old identified pattern: her strong need for feeling special to him and his guarded need not to be smothered or controlled by her. They had so positioned themselves in the marriage that each had to be right. They were not aware that the marriage always loses when marriage partners position themselves so that one wins, and the other loses. The couple had become stuck in their conflict, and the marriage was struggling for survival. In the initial sessions I worked with the couple to help them see their standoff and to encourage each to make an unguarded move toward the other. Jan was asked if she still believed her husband loved her. She replied, "I believe Mack loves me rationally, but I do not know if he loves me emotionally." In the sessions Mack had become annoyed and angry with Jan each time she had expressed her feelings of no longer being special to him. "I resent the fact that she has to ask me if I love her." Mack is a person who is strongly relational in need. That need is frustrated both by his unwillingness to share feelings and his lack of interest in listening to her feelings. He loves her, but he does not know how to communicate that love emotionally.

Emotionally, love is communicated through shared feelings. Love is far more than shared feelings, but without the intimacy produced when feelings are shared and received, love becomes too arid, functional, and factual. When a couple develops a comfort level with each other in which there is a mutual sharing of feelings (mad, sad, glad, and bad), that couple experiences the loving intimacy of relational living. In a relational marriage, each partner communicates a love that is both rational and emotional.

In a relational marriage, the full gamut of feelings is expressed. In a functional marriage, the feelings are there; they are just not acknowledged and certainly not cultivated. The one feeling that is often expressed is anger (mad). (This will be dealt with in the next chapter.) In the relational marriage, couples are more in tune with their feelings, and they express them. Tremendous potential for shared meaning exists: marital intimacy. When the four feelings (mad, sad, glad, and bad) are suppressed and withheld, they tend to pollute the personal system and then the marital system. To the contrary, sharing such feelings enables a couple to experience an immediate bond of support and closeness and to develop a relational security that fosters personal and marital vulnerability and growth.

Facts reveal what is happening to a person's life. Feelings reveal the reactions and responses in a person's life to those events. Feelings register the internal nature of a person, and facts are collected data that describe what is going on and what needs to be done to appropriately deal with a given situation. In a relational setting, whether in a marital or family one, feelings are valid. The need to acknowledge and express feelings is a vital component to the resolution of tension created by personal differences and to the process that moves toward the utilization of insight and mutual decision making. In a marital difference, feelings are always feet out front of facts. Too often in marriage, feelings are either ignored as unimportant or are bypassed on the way to rational resolution.

Feelings are too valid to either be ignored or bypassed. Functional relationships tend to ignore and bypass feelings because they are not perceived to be critical to marital conflict resolution. To the contrary, relational couples feed off the fruits produced by shared feelings that confirm and affirm their personal and relational value. Shared feelings diffuse the tension in a given situation and allow a couple to get to their resolution more clearly and quickly. Taking the time to acknowledge and express feelings gives the couple an opportunity to become involved with each other in a way that is both personally and maritally reassuring. All of these fruits produced by shared feelings in a marriage can be best summed up by the word *intimacy*. There is a closeness present that communicates the specialness of each and the value of the relationship to both.

For a couple in counseling or enrichment, personal history and the marital history are both important. History helps to clarify what belongs to the marriage and what belongs to the individuals prior to the marriage. Jack and Pam were seriously considering divorce, but before either was willing to call it quits and make that move, they agreed to seek marital counseling. After an hour with the couple it was obvious that her low self-esteem and his unresolved guilt related to his father's death were poisoning the marital relationship. Individual therapy was needed before they could be responsive to marital therapy.

The value of personal and marital history is critical for a second reason. It identifies the communication pattern of a couple prior to the present marital crisis. I have observed that couples who are children of the fifties and sixties usually approach marriage with relational intentions. They intend to have a relational marriage. Their communication patterns are indicative of that intention in that feelings are perceived as valid and are expressed. After they are married for a time, this often changes. The reasons for the change are many. (1) Sometimes other good things like jobs, children, friends, etc., become more important than the relationship. (2) After a while marriage loses its newness, and the growing "familiarity . . . breeds contempt." (3) Some couples are unable to take the differences that were mutually attractive in dating and courtship and integrate them into a working marital relationship. (4) Often unreal expectations partners have of each other never materialize.

The marital history is helpful in revealing whether or not the stress of marriage is due to the adjustments of marriage, the unresolved conflicts of marriage, or the frequent return by one or both to the premarital self in which communication was more factual and rational. The commitment of marriage either nurtures a developing self or causes one to retreat back into an old self. Since, generally, women are more open to and comfortable with feelings and expressing them, it is usually the husband who retreats back to a communication pattern in which feelings are not recognized or expressed. At this point, his past experiences are greater than his new intentions. Wives describe their frustrations these ways: "We don't know each other anymore"; "He is not interested or involved with me"; "He is a stranger to me"; "Our communication is just chitchat." If feelings were shared at one time in a marriage and then dissipated, it is due either to a return to a former pattern of communication by one or both or to differences that have not been integrated into the marital union, thus unresolved conflict.

Pat and John began their marriage with relational intentions. Early in the marriage Pat's need to feel special to John—a feeling she wanted but never got from her father—and John's fear of being consumed and controlled—a fear that was operative throughout his adolescence with his father—had collided, and they were stuck. Her need for more involvement and his need for distance created tension for Pat, and she wanted to share those feelings with John. John retreated into the safety and security of facts and functions, which he had used with his father as an adolescent. The result was Pat felt John's support rationally but not emotionally.

In both a relational and functional marriage, there is a predictable relationship between feelings and facts. In a functional marriage, feelings are ignored or suppressed, and the communication is almost totally factual and rational. How one feels is important only as those feelings are controlled and expressed in a way that helps to clarify the situation so that a workable solution can be reached. Feelings are denied so that the marital functions are not threatened, thwarted, or terminated. The marital functions are viewed as more valid and important than the marital relationship. Thus, to a functional marriage, the relationship between feelings and facts is one in which feelings are played down and ignored, and facts are expected.

There is a contrasting position between feelings and facts in a relational marriage. Feelings have priority over facts and are to be acknowledged and expressed as an important preliminary step toward insight and rational decisions. To ignore or bypass the feelings created by a given event or situation is, in a real sense, to reject the person. It tends to make the event or situation seem more important than the person. Since what one feels is out front and prior to what one thinks, to deal with feelings is the first step to clear thinking and good decision making. Thus feelings, in a relational marriage, are prior to and a valid part of resolution.

In a marriage relationship, a primary need is for someone to listen. A secondary need is to get help. When a couple moves to the secondary need without dealing with the primary need, the result is blocked communication. This is illustrated by the familiar story of the husband who comes home and finds his wife totally whipped by the day's care of three preschool children. She is ready to explode with controlled feelings. He steps into her world, evaluates the situation quickly, and says, "Let's get out of here. Let's go and get an ice cream cone." The ice cream cone is great if it is a means to an end, but not an end itself. The need is for a companion who sees her situation and offers her a listening ear, a supportive touch, and the time to understand. Her need is to share her feelings and to have a safe place and person with whom to "unchoke" and to regain her perspective and control.

The absence of shared feelings in a functional marriage does not significantly affect the established functions of that marriage. It can even enhance them. Not to talk out feelings in a relational marriage significantly limits the relationship. It affects that which is primary: the relationship itself.

Mary is a twenty-six-year-old woman who has recently divorced and who is involved in a new and serious relationship. One of her personal agendas that predated her marriage was her inability to make decisions. She grew up in a family where decisions had to be right because there was little room for error. To fail was unacceptable and almost unpardonable. Her first marriage had failed, and her family had worked it through to the point of acceptance, but the clear message was, "Not again." Still emotionally hooked into her family as a child, Mary was feeling trapped in her present relationship. She needed and appreciated Joe but was fearful of a commitment. She wanted to be married again, but she had to eliminate all possibilities of a second failure. In the trap, she became indecisive and behaved in a way to sabotage the relationship, thus her way out of the trap.

I had counseled with Mary and Jim and worked with them to see if they could build a relational marriage. Mary had assumed primary responsibility for the relationship, and Jim had given himself to hard work in order for them to enjoy life, something he had missed in his childhood and adolescent years. In the sessions, Mary

shared her feelings openly and fully, and Jim remained
distant and rational.

In counseling with Mary and Joe, it was most helpful
when I pointed out that in her marriage to Jim she had
wanted and pursued a relationship that Jim did not want.
In this new relationship, I saw both Joe and Mary wanting the same thing. They acknowledged their feelings and
listened to each other as they expressed how they felt.
Mary and Joe had established a good communication system in which differences were compromised, and decisions were made because they shared with each other
their feelings as they made mutually satisfying decisions
and resolutions. A marriage that is not free and comfortable with feelings is a marriage that is or will become a
functional one.

There is a rational process that most of us employ in
communicating at a functional level on a day-to-day basis. That process has four steps. First, there is an event.
Next, there is our perception of that event. We rationally
evaluate that event, and then, finally, we respond with
some kind of appropriate behavior. There is event, perception of the event, rational process, and appropriate
behavior.

This process is very valid as we seek to be appropriate
and responsible in the many roles that belong to each of
us in our families, our jobs, and our church and community life. This process is critical to our functional life.

There is a serious limitation to this four-step process in
our relational lives, particularly in marriage. A marital
relationship requires an additional step. There is the
event, our perception of that event, the feelings that result from our perception, our thoughts, and our behavior.
The additional step is the presence of our feelings that
result from our perception of the event. In a functional
process, one's feelings are present, but they are regarded

as less valid or not valid at all. They are not present, acknowledged, or dealt with as a valid step in the process. In a functional setting such as work, or in a functional marriage, the failure to accept, acknowledge, or deal with the feelings does not deter from the function. It usually enhances it.

For example, if an employee fails to perform a task as understood by the supervisor and is confronted with the failure, the feelings that both have as a result of their perception are not often spoken. Certainly, they are not viewed as necessary to whatever correction needs to be made to get done the stated task. The four-step communication process is a functional one.

In a relationship, the additional step is critical. Feelings must be recognized and expressed. The sharing of thought is opening up our minds. The sharing of feelings and thoughts is the opening up of our lives to each other. Thoughts without feelings hold a person off at a safe distance. Sharing feelings and thoughts is a willingness to be vulnerable to another in order to be known.

For example, a couple has an argument, and the following evening both still feel separated and afraid. From experience, both know that if they fail to share and deal with their feelings, they will eventually return to each other. In the meantime, they are together but feel separated. Their feelings left alone, they continue to function well. Finally she asks, "Can we talk?" "Sure," he replies. She then shares her feelings of anger at being put in the position where the initiative for reconciliation in their relationship is usually left up to her. He shares his feelings of fear of being rejected if he takes the initiative. Both their feelings are the result of their perceptions of a common event and history. When shared, their feelings allow them to move on through the communication process to a resolution. Sharing their feelings is not necessary for them to continue functioning in their respective roles. Sharing their feelings is necessary for them to have and keep a relationship that is open and honest. It frees them from being distant and separated and allows them to be close again and intimate.

Couples who share their feelings as a valid step in their communication experience a relational intimacy that is absent and, I believe, impossible for couples who share only rationally and factually.

Relational/Functional Exercise

Using the five-noted characteristics contrasting a relational and functional marriage, each marriage partner is to evaluate his or her marriage as relational or functional. The scale is one to ten, ten being the maximum relational. Give first your own perception of how you see the marriage, and then give your perception of how your partner sees the marriage.

Functional   Relational

1	2	3	4	5	6	7	8	9	10
								h	w

1. Change versus sameness
2. Communication: feelings vs. facts

Communication: Feelings and Facts

1. Answer the following questions based on your perceptions of your marriage:
1. Which partner tends to communicate more factually?
2. Which partner tends to express feelings?
3. In expressing feelings (mad, sad, glad, and bad), which one gets expressed most?

(In scoring, use 100 pounds)

Husband	Wife
mad	mad
sad	sad
glad	glad
bad	bad

2. Our communication patterns are learned ones. All of us are highly influenced by the communication patterns we saw in our families. It is easy for us to reproduce those patterns and more difficult for us to change them. The first step to change is to identify our own patterns and where they originated. As a couple do the following exercise and then share it:

In my family (parents, siblings, and grandparents, etc.) the person who most displayed each of the following feelings was:

Husband:
  Mad:
  Sad:
  Glad:
  Bad:
Wife:
  Mad:
  Sad:
  Glad:
  Bad:

After identifying the people in your family who most expressed each feeling, share with each other how the emotions were acted out and how the acting out made you feel.

3. In order to become more aware of your feelings and then practice sharing them, find a time each week to

share with each other when you felt sad, glad, bad, or
mad.

Husband:

    I felt sad when:

    I felt glad when:

    I felt bad when:

    I felt mad when:

Wife:

    I felt sad when:

    I felt glad when:

    I felt bad when:

    I felt mad when:

4. Learning from Scripture: Feelings

Each of the passages identify an experience when a person felt either bad, glad, sad, or mad.

Identify the feeling and then the cause of that particular feeling.

    Passage 1: Psalm 8

    Passage 2: Psalm 51:1-9

    Passage 3: Matthew 21:12-13

    Passage 4: John 11:17-37

6

Conflict Resolution Versus Unresolved Conflict

Conflict resolution is the process by which the emotion of anger that is potentially destructive is channeled into behavior that is personally and relationally constructive and redemptive.

A relational marriage is one in which unresolved conflict is addressed and resolved because the relationship is significantly restricted by the feelings of distance and separation. In a functional marriage, unresolved conflict is not only tolerated but often created to nurture distance and separation, which can be used to both justify and to energize the functional roles of marriage. In the heat of battle a husband says to his wife, "I might as well stay late at work. Why come home to someone who treats me like a stranger?" A wife may react by seeking from her career, children, church, or community the involvement that she wants and needs from a relational husband. Married couples not only have limited understanding in how to resolve conflict, but they often use unresolved conflict to protect their functional selves and roles. To resolve conflict a couple needs help in knowing how to do it appropriately and effectively.

For example, if you want to learn to dive, you seek out the best diving coach you can find. The coach gives instructions in the art of diving. You watch the films, listen to the tapes, and perfect the art, but you are afraid of the water. Ultimately, diving and water are essentially wedded to each other, and you have to be comfortable with both. Couples who respond well to learning how to resolve conflict (the diving) are well established in their own person (the water); they are open to a relational marriage.

Conflict resolution is an open, up-front agenda in the biblical record. It began early in the creation event when Adam and Eve, as individuals and as representatives of all manhood and womanhood, made choices out of their differences and experienced separation and isolation. Neither was willing to take responsibility for his or her behavior, and they remained separated because they chose to blame rather than to resolve. Cain and Abel followed suit and sought to resolve their differences by fighting. Abel was killed, and Cain went to live in the land of Nod, which means "to wander."

Isaac and Rebekah had differing opinions about their twin sons, Esau and Jacob. Isaac favored Esau because he was the firstborn. Rebekah loved and favored Jacob. Their personal favorites produced unresolved conflicts between them that were translated into a dramatic scheme of trickery, leaving the two brothers estranged. Esau was left with revenge and Jacob with a fear of his brother. The two brothers eventually did what their parents had failed to do. They resolved their differences. Jacob faced his fear and came home to meet Esau. Esau faced his revenge and received Jacob openly. The resolution of their conflict is the foundational stone of the biblical understanding of reconciliation. This understanding is fully matured in the apostle Paul's words, "In Christ God was reconciling the world to himself" (2 Cor. 5:19).

In between the Esau-Jacob episode and Paul's words are the teachings of Christ on conflict resolution. From the radical command to settle differences by turning "the other cheek" to the practical advice to resolve conflict by taking the initiative toward the one who has offended you

(Matt. 5:21-26), to seeking the help of a third party to assist in the conflict resolution if the different parties are unable to resolve it themselves (Matt. 18:15-17), Jesus both encouraged and demanded conflict resolution from His followers.

Relational living creates conflict, whether on the vertical level between God and humanity or on the horizontal level between person and person. The difference between relational and functional living is not the absence of conflict but the way the conflict is handled and resolved.

In marriage, the sources of conflict are primarily twofold. First, there is the matter of differences (see exercise at end of chapter). In courtship, we usually are attracted to persons who are different from us in some significant ways. I recall as a young lad one of my most-treasured toys was a set of dogs, one white and the other black, which had magnets in their base. I spent hours playing with them. When I placed the ends that were negatively and positively charged toward each other, I had a difficult time keeping the dogs apart—they were attracted to each other. If I placed the likes together, the dogs moved apart and never could quite catch up with each other.

Differences do attract because in courtship and marriage we do not look for a clone. That would be too much! We look for someone to complement us so that we are made more full and complete. Those things that we seek in each other to complete us in marriage are the same things that cause friction and conflict. For example, my wife grew up in a family where her parents were very demonstrative in their affection to their children and they in return to them. As a young man, I was particularly aware of her father! In courting Sydnor, I was enthralled by the continued affection she and her father shared as they took walks together, sat on the couch and held

hands, and talked about personal as well as national issues. What they had, I soon envisioned our having, and I
dreamed that I as a father would have such a relationship
with my daughter.

I, on the other hand, grew up in a family where love
was present, but it was communicated primarily by doing
something for another. My dad was a provider. My mom
was one who took great pride in making sure we were
well fed, well scrubbed, and well behaved. There was not
much time or much understood need for affection, for
hugs, or for "I love you." From my parents I learned well
how to do for but not so well how to be with. While I was
courting, I increased my ability to give affection, but after
I got married I returned to my normal state. In marriage,
my wife expected me to be as affectionate as her father;
thus, early in our marriage, she experienced some rejection while I experienced some smothering. Our difference, which in courtship was tempered, became conflict
producing in marriage.

A second source of conflict is that of unmet needs. To
need is not in and of itself selfish. To need and expect that
need to be met when and how we want and expect it to be
is selfish. Again, my wife came into marriage with a
much higher need level for affection, and that unmet
need was conflict producing. On the other hand, I came
into the marriage with a much greater need for space.
When that need was unmet, I quickly and efficiently became adept at setting up conflict as a way to get the need
met.

Each person is a being with many needs. We have psy-
chological needs, such as love, acceptance, security, and
belonging; we have physical needs, such as food, clothing,
shelter, and sex; and we have spiritual needs, such as forgiveness, salvation, service, and worship. In marriage, a
couple brings all of these needs to each other. All of the

needs of one person can never be met by any other person. Yet, the marriage relationship has as its primary role that of meeting the needs of each other. Family, friends, peers, and church and community acquaintances are significant but secondary.

In marriage, the differences that in courtship and early marriage attracted now irritate, and the needs that are real and legitimate but go unmet produce conflict. Conflict is the state of affairs, and anger is the present emotion. In marriage, conflict resolution is the process by which the potentially destructive emotion of anger is channeled into behavior that is personally and relationally constructive and redemptive. Biblically, conflict resolution is the willingness of couples to implement Paul's definition of love:

> Love is patient and kind; love is not jealous or boastful; it is not arrogant or rude. Love does not insist on its own way; it is not irritable or resentful; it does not rejoice at wrong, but rejoices in the right. Love bears all things, believes all things, hopes all things, endures all things (1 Cor. 13:4-7).

Four emotions characterize our relational living: mad, sad, glad, and bad. Mad is the feeling we are most familiar with, and it is also the one with which we are most uncomfortable and most irresponsible. This is particularly true of Christians. We are familiar with it in that we feel it and know it, but we are not good at being creative and constructive with it.

Much of this is due to either the incorrect teaching of the church or the lack of distinction between feeling anger and expressing anger. The feeling of anger we cannot control. The expression of anger we must control. We are not responsible for feeling anger when differences are present or needs are unmet. We are always responsible for what we do with our anger. Jesus was angry at the Pharisees when they ascribed more good to keeping the sabbath than they did to healing a disabled man (Mark 3:5). Jesus was angry at the religious leaders who had taken the Temple built for worship and made it into a trading center (Matt. 21:12). If Jesus were perfect—and He was—and if He were angry—and He was—then the sin is not in the feeling of anger but in the misuse and abuse of anger. Given the situations, Jesus neither misused nor abused His anger.

Marriage, because of its close proximity, is an incubator of anger. It is a relationship different from all other relationships. If a couple has a serious and strong commitment to the institution and walking out or breaking out are not viable options for resolving conflict, then it is essential that couples learn to recognize and handle anger. When we participate in a friendship, and anger is present due to differences or unmet needs, there is much more built-in space and mobility than in marriage. Even when couples are angry with each other, they still eat together, sleep together, and go to church together.

As a teenager, one of my jobs was to periodically help my dad and brothers shell corn. The corn sheller was operated by hand, and the handle that turned the cogs worked smoothly and easily as long as there was no corn. Once the ear of corn was dropped in place, the tension necessary to shell the corn became greater and more demanding. So it is in marriage. The cogs that run continuously in marriage to produce the marital "meal" are constantly engaged. Tension and friction are indigenous to the relationship.

The close proximity, the personal differences, the meeting of needs, and the strong commitment persons make to marriage all combine to produce a ripe setting for anger. It is critical that a couple know this, expect this, and learn how to handle anger. Resolving anger in marriage is critical because of the tendency couples have to collect anger. When anger is present in marriage, the one who feels it must assume primary responsibility for the anger and take the initiative to resolve it. The other partner must be responsive to that initiative and assume joint and equal responsibility for the relationship. Where one often takes responsibility for the anger, both must always assume responsibility for what affects or interferes with the marital relationship.

To whom much is given, much is required. Since marriage, by its creative use of tension, produces anger, it is necessary that couples deal with anger when it occurs. It does not always have to be done immediately, but usually the result is best when the resolution is near the cause and source of the anger. In order to keep the issues identified, and in order to keep the anger in direct proportion to the cause or event, anger needs to be dealt with and resolved as it occurs. Not to deal with anger currently is to collect the anger. Then the marriage has to deal with a low-grade marital fever, or it has to face and to recover from periodic explosions.

Many persons are hesitant to verbalize and claim their anger. This is seen in the need to call it by other names. Persons say, "I am irritated," "frustrated" "put out with," or "mad." The word *anger*, for some, has become more acceptable, but for many, especially church folks, it is still more comfortably labeled by other words.

Four Faces of Anger

Anger is an emotion that has many different faces. The emotion is one, but the faces are different in terms of intensity. The progression of the emotion from low intensity to high intensity would be as follows:

Irritation   anger   resentment   hate

Irritation

When one partner says of the other, "I get so irritated with him," she is talking about the emotion *anger*. The intensity level usually is slight, and the source is some personal peculiarity, idiosyncrasy, or habit, such as squeezing the tube of toothpaste in the middle, leaving cabinet doors open, leaving lights on, or of eating slowly (or rapidly). Couples who work at accepting, overlooking, or integrating these personal peculiarities into their marriage deal with anger at the initial level. In the words of the song, "Little things do mean a lot"!

Anger

When there is a specific event in which we feel hurt, rejected, or disappointed, the intensity level is heightened and we feel angry. For example, the budget had clearly designated a certain amount for recreation, and the husband had knowingly overspent the budget. The wife felt angry because the husband had been lax in his commitment to a mutually accepted agreement. Or, the wife was ready for an appointed occasion, and the husband watched the last quarter of a football game. These situations are common to marital life. We ignored or withheld what we knew our partner expected, needed, or wanted, and our spouse felt angry. In this stage of anger, those events happen frequently enough that the anger cannot be handled by the process of osmosis. Anger does tend to diffuse, slowly dissipate, or work its way out. Our personal systems are made to get angry in order to fight or take flight but not to stay angry. When couples do not address the sources of their anger, the anger is too frequently produced to be resolved by the often-chosen process of osmosis. Thus, there is the cumulative effect.

Resentment

Resentment is anger that is frozen, solidified, or concretized. Resentment is what naturally occurs in a relationship when couples do not acknowledge and resolve their anger. This resentment becomes a wall that either slowly or quickly separates the couple so that they are trapped in an institution, a form that has little or no substance.

Resentment in marriage is like a wall, and it usually grows slowly. Since the relationship is a living, dynamic entity, so is the wall. It grows something like this:

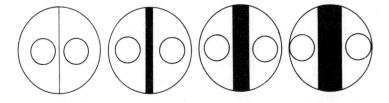

The wall of resentment denies and obstructs a relationship. It is not only allowed, it frequently is used by the partners to nurture and justify stronger commitments to respective roles and functions.

Hate

In marriage, where there is close proximity, strong commitment to the institution, unresolved anger, and the intention to win either by attack or by retreat, couples can and do reach a state where they hate each other. Hate has built into it the intention to hurt.

The partners, at first friends and now enemies, seek

ways to hurt each other. One of the most descriptive portrayals of hate in marriage is the play and movie *Who's Afraid of Virginia Woolf?* (Edward Albee). Both play and film are about Martha and George, a middle-aged couple in a college community, who expose their marital cynicism and hate to the world. It is a marriage described by David H. C. Read as "cleverness without compassion, of wit without humor, of passion without values, of fantasy unredeemed by faith."[1] Sometimes marital institutions are preserved to become incubators of hate where persons become animal-like in their behavior. It is probably here more than any other place where people experience "hell on earth."

Anger is powerful energy. When it is channeled and used creatively and redemptively, it feeds and nurtures a growing marriage. When anger is allowed to chart its own course in marriage, it cuts away and bruises; it attacks and destroys; it blocks and bottles so that marriages and persons become its casualty.

Married couples employ a variety of ways to deal with their conflict and anger. In response or reaction to an issue, couples can move over, away, against, or through conflict.

Over	Away	Against	Through
$X = \dfrac{0}{0}$	X – 0→0→0	~~0 X 0~~	$\begin{array}{c} 00 \\ X \end{array}$

(X = the event, O = the response to the event.)

The first position is one in which one partner assumes an over position, taking control of the situation. In the second position one partner pursues, and the other retreats. In the third, the issue is bypassed or used as the partners position themselves to go against each other. In the fourth, the couple maintains a side-by-side position so as to attack the issue and not each other; they confront the issue and work through it. Only one, the fourth, conflict resolution, allows and supports a relational marriage. The other three are found in functional marriages. Unresolved conflict blocks a relational style of marriage, but it survives and often lives well in a functional style of marriage.

Four Ways of Handling Conflict

Do Not Allow Conflict

Some marriages seek to handle conflict by not allowing it. Sometimes a marital partner will say, "I never heard or saw my parents fight." This does not mean that they did not. It usually means that they chose not to fight openly or directly. The anger was there, but it was either not allowed, not accepted, or bottled and stored away.

In generations past, in the traditional marriages where the husband was dominant and the wife submissive, the husband claimed his authority by the nature of his position and did not allow openly for differences of opinions, dialogue, or equal time. My father was of this vintage. It worked better with his children than it did with his wife. Of the nine children, there was only one who had rather "bear the rod" than hold his tongue. In our family there was little open confrontation or conflict between my father and the children. There was a lot of undercover anger that left jobs undone or half done, that talked back when he was gone, and that fostered, for some, a rebellious desire to leave home as early as possible. My father was in charge, and we knew it. Only occasionally was he challenged, and each time the results further established him in that solitary position. In our family, like many families of the 1930s, forties, and fifties, conflict was not resolved. It was not allowed. The marriage and the family were highly functional and only slightly relational.

Attack and Retreat

A second way that couples handle their marital conflict is that of attack and retreat. In this style, one person is out in the open, and the other is hidden; one is active, and the other is passive; one tends to fight, and the other pouts. The more frustrated of the two is usually the fighter. Imagine, if you will, two boxers who are primed for a fight. They both arrive early, weigh in, and wait anxiously for the fight. On the evening of the fight, at the scheduled hour, one boxer leaves his dressing room and enters the ring where he dances and spars, waiting for his opponent to show. He dances and paces and looks expectantly for his foe. His foe, in the meantime, is back in his dressing room, dressed, primed, but with no intention to show and fight. Who actually wins the bout? In boxing, the fighter who shows is awarded the win by default. In marriage, the opposite is true. The winner is the one who does not show, who stays in the dressing room safely out of sight and reach. In relational terms, the person who does not show is labeled as passive aggressive. It is hard to fight and impossible to whip a person who is passive aggressive in a fighting style. This style seldom wins by a knockout but by default.

Men, more so than women, employ this fighting technique. There are several reasons for this. Men generally are more closed and private with their feelings. The feeling of anger is no exception. Even though it is the feeling most frequently shown, men suppress their anger and divert it into passive aggressive behaviors, such as being late, choosing to leave chores undone, watching television, or reading, or not talking.

Men, as boys, learned early how to get space from their mothers—withhold the information that she needs or wants. "Where did you go last night, son?" she asks. "Oh, nowhere special." "Who were you with?" "Just some friends," he answers. "How was the test?" "About like the last one." The space he needs and wants is more space than his mother needs and wants. Occasionally, explosions occur, but more often it is silence and secrecy. Since men are boys grown up, and wives are at times perceived to be and related to as mothers, the same technique is used. Since the setting is similar and the characters somewhat the same, the expectation is that the same technique can and will produce the same results: space. When men are passive aggressive in their behaviors, they are adolescent adults who are not yet sure there is another or better way to get space.

A third reason why husbands use the retreat technique in marital conflict is that men fear getting out of control with their anger if they stay and fight. As boys they were strongly encouraged not to be bullied but to physically fight to hold their ground. What was encouraged and strongly programmed for boys is no longer accepted. So husbands in the midst of marital conflict withdraw and retreat as a way to maintain control of their anger.

A fourth reason that some men retreat with their feelings of anger is they perceive that women are better at knowing and expressing feelings than they are. Thus, men keep and retreat with their feelings as a way to avoid personal threat, intimidation, or defeat. Some wives use and employ retreat as a way of expressing anger. The results are the same—a more functional marriage or a conflictual marriage.

Fight

Some couples deal with conflict by fighting. The intent is not to settle anything. The fighting serves several purposes. First, it lances the marital boil and drains off the accumulated buildup of collected anger. Secondly, it is for some couples the only intimacy they share. The opposite of intimacy is to ignore or disregard. Just as a child will not be ignored, a marriage will not be either. A fight is the reassurance that each partner will not and cannot be ignored. A third reason that couples fight is that a fight is one of the ways partners signal to each other that nothing has changed. It is a way to reassure each other that the respective positions in the marriage are intact and remain the same.

Resolve the Conflict

The fourth way to handle conflict is to work through it—resolve it. Most couples employ the first three ways for differing reasons. Those who establish themselves in functional marriages find that they can more easily continue without interruption when unresolved conflict is present. Other couples choose one of the first three (over, away, or against) because they are familiar with them. They have seen them modeled at home, at work, at school, etc. For most couples, conflict resolution is still an uncharted sea. It is one of the most critical needs facing marriages, and couples are eager to find a way to do it.

Before detailing a method to use in conflict resolution, there are several basic needs that a couple must establish before they approach conflict resolution. First, the couple must have a desire to have a relational marriage and a commitment to make it happen. Second, a high trust level is needed so that partners feel and know that their spouse and their relationship are more important than selfishly having one's own way. Third, both partners consciously recognize that feelings are important and need to be expressed and heard. Fourth, in the conflict resolution, the issues—not the person—are addressed and attacked. One way to visually demonstrate the importance of attacking issues and not persons is to take three chairs, place two side by side, and set the third directly in front of the two. Have the couple sit in the two chairs and face the third chair, appropriately tagged "issue or cause of the conflict." This way they are partners together addressing an issue on which they differ.

Four Steps to Resolving Conflict

Couples want and need a clear, simple, workable method to address and resolve conflict. A method that best meets these criteria is one suggested by Dr. David and Vera Mace.[2] It is a four-step process:

Step One

In the absence of conflict, the couple makes a contract with each other that they will not attack each other. This step is basic because it establishes a ground rule that has to be present and honored in order for the plan to work. Since partners in marriage are best friends, the contract underscores the friendship by agreeing that attacking each other is unacceptable. The contract not to attack permits the partners to stay away from a defensive position, to be safe when anger is shared, and to be free to be better listeners. The contract is a statement, such as, "Since you are my best friend, in our conflict resolution I promise not to attack you but to confront and attack the source of the anger." To live by the contract, either partner who feels attacked at any time has permission to put up his or her hand and say, "I'm feeling attacked. Can you say it another way?" The speaker always hears and honors the request. It is important that partners not use the request unfairly.

Step Two

The person with the anger has the responsibility to approach the other partner to schedule the time to deal with the anger. This is important for several reasons. It eliminates the assumption that if one partner is angry, the other party knows it. It makes the angry partner responsible for his or her feelings. It places responsibility on the partner who is feeling angry to take the initiative to schedule time to resolve the anger. It is critical that scheduled time be made. Often the anger can be dealt with when it is first acknowledged. If the anger is too strong and time is needed to lower the temperature, claim the time and space, but at the same time make a clearly-stated appointment with each other to get to the anger. The scheduling of the time reassures the one feeling anger that both the person and the anger are valid. Feeling that the anger is not going to be ignored or treated lightly, the partner is reassured, and this allows for postponement. The permission to postpone also acknowledges that life cannot always be stopped at the very moment one needs for it to stop. Once again, it is important that postponement not be used unfairly.

Step Three

Reflective listening is listening without interpreting, editing, or altering. It is reflecting back what is said so that the speaker is satisfied that he or she has been heard. This allows the speaker a captive audience of one and frees the listener from taking a defensive position. The partner who is angry about a particular issue expresses that anger as clearly and as briefly as possible. The other partner listens, reflecting back what is said until the partner says, "Yes. That is how I feel." The speaking partner then becomes the listening partner as they exchange roles. The speaking partner expresses how he feels about the issue and about what was expressed. The speaking/ listening exchange continues until both persons have shared their feelings. The primary purpose of stage three is to defuse the anger, which then places the couple in a better position to use a rational process to resolve the conflict.

Step Four

Conflict resolution is a process of communication in which a couple moves from event, to perception of the event, to feelings, to rational thinking, and, finally, to decision. When the anger is defused, the couple is positioned then to use their abilities to work out a profitable resolution. The resolution that favors one but satisfies both is acceptable if no pattern is established that leans predominantly in one direction.

Two Case Studies of Resolved Conflict

Kim and Kevin

In a marriage enrichment event using the conflict resolution process, a couple shared with the group how their differing philosophies about money had been a frequent source of anger and conflict. Kim and Kevin had been married for eighteen years. Her family background was one in which money was not plenteous, but it was available and meant to be spent. Kim was given her own money, and she had control over it and freedom to use it. She was responsible with her money, which, in turn, kept money available. Kevin's family was one that had enough money for essentials but little or no excess money. Kevin's personal money was either sparingly given by his parents or earned. He, too, was responsible. Money was to be spent for necessities and then saved for a rainy day. A nest egg that represented security for Kevin was not an extra but an essential.

In the marriage, both Kim and Kevin were responsible with money. They both worked, and money was, once again, not plenteous but available. Money to Kim was to be responsibly spent and enjoyed. For Kevin, money was to be used for necessities, but extra money was to be saved. Their differing philosophies about money brought to their marriage a potential source of conflict, and in marriage it had been a primary source of anger and conflict. In the marriage enrichment group, they shared a facet of this conflict, using the process of conflict resolution.

Step 1. After participating in a marriage enrichment event, Kim and Kevin had made a contract not to attack each other, and they had sought to live by that contract.

Step 2. Kevin was the one feeling angry about how a recent part of their financial agreement had been handled, so he took the initiative in scheduling a time to deal with his feelings and their issue.

Step 3. Kevin spoke, and Kim listened. "In our discussions about plans to handle our money, we agreed that I would keep the checking-account balance book, and you would post the checks you had written in my book daily or keep them current. I feel angry with you that just recently you did not post your checks for over a week, and when you did, I realized that we had far less money than our balance showed. There were some pending bills due, and to my surprise, there wasn't enough money to cover them. I was angry about the situation, about not being able to pay the bills, and at you for not living by our agreement."

Kim reflected back what she heard Kevin say and feel. "I heard you say that you felt angry about my not living by our agreement to keep the checks current in the balance book, and that you were angry for being in a situation where there was not enough money to pay the bills."

Kevin responded, "Yes, that is what I said, and that's how I feel."

At this point in the process, the partners changed roles. Kevin was the reflective listener, and Kim shared her feelings. "I realize that I did not keep our agreement. That is my fault, and I accept responsibility for it. I also feel that I have gotten too little credit for my efforts at keeping the agreement. I feel that my negligence one time does not cancel out my other efforts. I am working through it, but I still feel that I am accountable to you for how and when I spend money."

Kevin listened and responded to what he heard Kim say: "I heard you say that you accept responsibility for not keeping our agreement. You also feel that I'm overlooking your concerted effort to keep your checks posted, and you still feel parented in how and when you spend money." Kim confirms that she has been heard.

Kevin continued, "When you don't keep our agreement, I fear that the old pattern of your not posting your checks will return. I also feel that I'm put in a position to parent, and I don't like that."

Kim reflected what Kevin said, "You are not yet sure I accept or will keep the agreement. You also feel that sometimes I still put you in the parenting role."

"You heard me."

Kim and Kevin continued twice more to speak and listen and to clear the air with their feelings and to defuse their anger.

Step 4. The anger defused, Kim and Kevin are better positioned to reaffirm their agreement. They can decide to continue to be mutually supportive of their efforts to deal with past histories regarding money and their desire to integrate their differences into their marital relationship.

Vic and Vickie

Vic and Vickie have been married six years. They have one child, Jennifer, age two. Both work at jobs that are stressful. Vickie is a nurse, and Vic is a stockbroker. They are highly motivated to have a good marriage, and they have participated in marriage enrichment several times.

During a marriage enrichment retreat, Vic and Vickie were asked to role-play conflict resolution. They were to bring their own agenda, one that was recent and recurring.

Their agenda was household duties. Early in their marriage they had agreed that since both of them worked equally outside the home, they would share equally their duties inside the home. On paper the contract was made and kept. In practice, Vic, influenced by his family background in which roles were clearly defined as masculine and feminine, reneged when he and Vickie got home in the evening tired, stressed, and spent. It was easy for Vic to disregard the agreement and leave most of the household duties to Vickie. For the sake of peace, Vickie would allow him that privilege but with suppressed anger. The anger usually expressed itself passively and indirectly, but periodically her anger became more intense. The pattern was one of agreement, default on Vic's part, and conflict, but no resolution.

After confirming the contract not to attack, Vickie began the conflict-resolution process by claiming her anger.

"I feel that we made a contract that has little validity. We honor it for a while, and then we disregard it. When we do, I feel like the household duties are automatically assigned to me. You expect me to take over and treat you like your mom treated you. She didn't work at a job outside the home, and I do."

At this point, Vic shot up his hand indicating that he felt attacked. He expressed his feelings that Vickie moved away from her feelings and the issue and that she attacked him through use of a sensitive subject: his mother.

In expressing her feelings, it would have worked better if Vickie had used "I" messages instead of "you" messages. For example, "When this happened, I felt used and abandoned; and I felt angry about it." With these corrections, they moved on.

Vic repeated back to Vickie what she said she felt. "You feel I treat our mutually agreed-on contract lightly. It works for a while, and when it goes, I act as if the duties automatically belong to you."

Vickie replied, "Yes, that's true. That's how I feel."

"On paper, I do accept our contract," continued Vic. "I do take advantage of you because it's hard for you to let things slide. When we are both beat and tired, some things could be left undone, but you feel that they have to be done, and I don't always agree with that. Why don't we just pay somebody to do it?"

Vic responded with his feelings and did that well. Then he made a critical mistake. In the midst of sharing his feelings, he announced a quick solution. This indicates impatience with the process, thus rejecting both Vickie and the process. Vic was saying, "I don't have time for this, and our relationship is not that important." Furthermore, Vic made a quick, subtle move that is frequently made by persons who are more comfortable with the rational than they are with the emotional. He made a move to bypass, leap over feelings, and offer a resolution. He was more interested in fixing than he was in feelings.

Vickie reflected his feelings, "You do agree to our contract on paper, but often, when you are tired, you opt out and leave the duties to me. You feel some things could be left undone, but I have a hard time doing that, and you sometimes have to pay for it."

"Yeah! That's how I feel," Vic agreed.

Vickie continued, "You always have an answer." Vic's hand shot up. The "you" message and the disallowed word *always* combined to score a lick below the belt. "It is true that I have a hard time letting some things go. But I feel if I do, it will just snowball, and I will lose control. I could more easily let some things go if I felt you would help me later."

Vic repeated what he had heard, "You do accept that you have a hard time letting some things slide, but the reason for it is that you feel you will lose control. You feel that if you knew I would be there to help you later, you could let some of it go."

"Yes, that's true," Vickie said.

"I do feel we both are somewhat unreal in terms of what we expect. I feel we are under pressure most of the time to be a good partner, to parent well, and to be good at our jobs. I feel that all of this keeps getting to us."

"You feel we are both unrealistic about our expectations: that we live under constant stress."

"Yes, that's right," Vic agreed.

"I still feel it is hard for you to accept the tasks around the house because it is different from what you saw growing up. It is going to take a will to do it if we are going to work this out."

"You feel that doing my fair share around the house is not easy for me since I grew up in a family where the household tasks were done by Mom, and I will have to work at it."

"That's how I see it."

Vic said, "I mentioned earlier that one way we could take some of the pressure off of us would be to get outside help to come in and do part of the work. I am open to that and would be willing for us to pay for it."

At this point feelings have been expressed and heard. The anger has been defused. Vic and Vickie are ready to discuss some options and make a decision regarding a change needed to address the recurring issue that has been sensitive and conflict producing for them.

Vickie responded, "I like your suggestion. Can we afford it? Would you like for me to make some calls and get prices from some cleaning services?"

"That sounds good. You do that, and we can work it out. I feel good about it."

"Me, too. I have one other question: This won't be a substitute for your part in our agreement, will it?"

Vic reassured Vickie, "No. I want to do my part, and I will work on it and do better."

"Good."

This process of conflict resolution is a process that works. Couples who observe the process via role-playing in marriage enrichment events feel it to be unnatural and staged. Follow-up on couples after marriage enrichment events often reveals the same feelings. That is to be understood. It is so much more natural to express anger in an attacking or retreating way. Learned behavior (attacking, retreating, and fighting) that is more spontaneous and propagated by many visible models makes a more deliberate, unnatural approach (channeling anger creatively and constructively) appear strange and affected. Couples who have been consistent and intentional about using the process of conflict resolution report good results. They feel they have a handle on and control of a very critical marital issue.

Change in any area of life is slow. To believe in change and to make a commitment to it is one of the clearest indications that couples are mutually serious about marital growth—about creating and sustaining a relational marriage.

Conflict resolution in marriage is not optional. It is required for couples who want a relational marriage.

Relational/Functional Exercise

Using the five-noted characteristics contrasting a relational and functional marriage, each marriage partner is to evaluate the marriage as relational or functional. The scale is one to ten, ten being the maximum relational. Give first your own perception of how you see the marriage, and then give your perception of how your partner sees the marriage.

Functional   Relational
1   2   3   4   5   6   7   8   9   10

                                                   h   w

1. Change versus Sameness
2. Communication: Feelings Versus Facts
3. Conflict Resolution Versus Unresolved Conflict

Conflict Resolution Versus Unresolved Conflict

1. In marriage most conflict centers around the following basic marital issues. Use this exercise to separately prioritize these issues as to the source of conflict in your marriage. First, answer how you view conflict in your marriage, and, then, how you perceive your partner views it.

After you individually complete the exercise, share it with each other.

	Wife	Husband

1. Money
2. Children
3. Family (in-laws)
4. Sex
5. Friends
6. Household tasks
7. Recreation (hobby, etc.)
8. Work (profession, job, etc.)

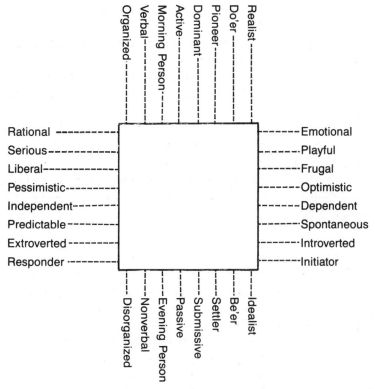

2. Instructions: Listed in the diagram above are some of

the differences that attract couples to each other and then in marriage often become the primary source of conflict. You and your partner separately should select three differences you feel are present in your marriage. This gives a possible number of six or a minimum number of three. Share with each other the differences selected and talk about how they have been integrated, compromised, into your marriage.

3. As adults, how we handle conflict is highly influenced by the way we saw conflict handled in our families. Share with your partner the way conflict was handled by your parents.

A. "Over" One parent assumed power and control and did not allow any conflict.

B. "From" One parent sought to deal with the conflict, but the other parent retreated or withdrew and would not talk or deal.

C. "Against" Issues produced conflict, and there was fighting where each attacked the other. Conflict was often present but seldom resolved.

D. "With" Conflict was present and out in the open. Each had feelings and opinions, and they were expressed and respected.

4. Learning from Scripture: Conflict

The following biblical passages demonstrate the ways conflict is approached and handled. Identify which one of the four ways (over, away from, against, or with) and share with each other the results.

Passage 1: Genesis 4:1-16
Passage 2: 1 Kings 21:1-16
Passage 3: Genesis 3:8-13
Passage 4: Genesis 33:1-11

Notes

1. David H. C. Read, *Virginia Woolf Meets Charlie Brown* (Grand Rapids: Eerdman, 1968), 91.

2. Dr. David Mace, *We Can Have Better Marriages.*

7

Intimacy Versus Sex

Sex is the thermometer that registers the temperature of the marriage.

Sex is a thermometer that registers the temperature of a marriage. It is often the first identified problem verbalized by a couple in marital counseling. The reason for that is clear. A couple is often more aware and in touch with the dissatisfaction of their sexual expression or of the noticeable changes that occur in their sex life. If, for example, the frequency of sexual intercourse takes a nose dive or an upswing, both partners tag that and ask questions either privately or of each other. The sexual act is more predictable and observable, but the marital issues that affect the sexual life of a couple are more hidden and complex.

In functional marriages, couples tend to have only sex. In relational marriages, sex is an expression of marital intimacy. In functional marriages, sex is an end within itself. In relational marriages, sex often is the completion of intimacy. A couple can have sex without intimacy. They can, and do, experience intimacy without sex. Sex takes only a few minutes while intimacy takes an evening or a good part of it. One of the more observable clues as to whether a marriage is functional or relational is whether sex is an act, a function, or the expression of intimacy. Functional sex in marriage involves two bodies and a brief moment. Intimacy requires far more. Intimacy requires a growing relationship.

Sex in marriage becomes all-important when it is either absent or unsatisfying to one or both of the partners. In early marriage, sex is centrally focused as to its importance in the relationship. With time, sex becomes less focused but not less important. In premarital counseling, it is important that couples understand the changing focus of sex in marriage. It can be clearly and helpfully shown by the following diagram:

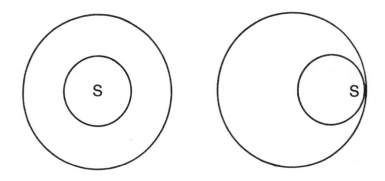

In the first circle, sex is centrally located. In the second circle, sex has moved over to the side, occupying its place among other valid and important expressions of marriage. Sex returns to the center each time it occurs.

In premarriage, couples should view sex as that part of the relationship that is desired but not permitted. In early marriage, sex is desirable and available. Waiting for what they wanted and now enjoying what they waited for makes sex central. After several months of marriage, sex slowly moves off center stage and occupies a place out in the wings. This in no way means that sex is less important. Its frequency usually decreases, but the joy and meaning of marital sex stays vibrant and alive. It is central as an expression of marital love rather than as a new marital experience.

A good sexual relationship in marriage is more of an art than a science. All the essentials are present, so a couple can experience sex as both a highly pleasurable experience and as one of the best and fullest ways to know and to love another. Many couples approach marital sex as a science rather than an art. As a science, the expectation is: there is a right way to use the essentials to produce an acceptable product and satisfied customer. Science tends to approach sex as a function, a job, a task, or a duty. Knowledge of the equipment and how to use it is central. There is certainly a place for science as persons are taught to understand, to accept, and to be comfortable with their bodies. A course in human sexuality is a "must" for couples who plan to be married. A thorough understanding of maleness and femaleness, of their similarities and differences, is foundational to a good, healthy sex life in marriage. Yet, it is possible to know all the facts, to have a good grasp of the science of sex, and still not find and experience the art of sex.

The art of sex is that which a couple creates with time and experience out of their own individual needs and differences. The artists are new and inexperienced, but they have an idea, a sketch, and a picture that is in process of being born. The canvas is new, and the colors are mixed. The sexual art that is created by the couple takes the essentials, adds time and experience, and produces a painting that is unique and mutually satisfying. Functional marriages tend to focus on sex as a science; relational marriages tend to focus on sex as an art.

Most marriages today begin with an intention and expectation to be relational. Some continue that way while most steer off course and follow a more functional path.

Even though the intention and the expectation in marriage is relational in need and hope, the dominant program for individuals in the American culture is that of function. As the marriage goes functional, so goes sex. Intimacy that was present in the initial stages of courtship and marriage either quickly or gradually diminishes, and it is replaced by the mere physical need and expression of sex. Couples often experience a sexual disappointment. They learn to accept far less than what is potentially present. What follows is what one husband cynically referred to as "the killing of a dream."

The results are varied. Some couples learn to expect no more than sex, and they build their marriage around sex as the expression of a physical need. Other couples push sex to the periphery of their marriage and divert the sexual energy and need into other good causes. Still other couples use sex as an instrument for marital warfare. Some couples, either one or both partners, are made vulnerable by the need and use that vulnerability to justify or to rationalize an extramarital relationship. The progression of estrangement evidenced in these marital options is often identified as a sexual problem. The sexual disappointment is a symptom initially and later remains a symptom, but, in addition, it has become a marital problem. In the same way that alcohol initially is a symptom that becomes a problem, sexual dissatisfaction is first a symptom and later a problem.

Marriage begins with a rather pure form of intimacy that has been untested in courtship. Ministers may ask couples who are planning to be married, "Why are you making this serious and permanent decision?" After recovering from the surprise of such a question, almost all answer, "Because we love each other, and we want to share our lives." And most of them do. However, the love they begin with is not deep enough or strong enough to bear the weight of years of marriage. If, as the weight increases, the love deepens and grows, then the weight is evenly divided, and it never becomes too great for the love. Marital love that is sufficient for the growing needs and demands of marriage has to be both relational and functional. However, it is the relational love that meets and nurtures the personal and the couple's need for intimacy.

Intimacy shared by a couple in marriage is a gift that began before marriage and continues in marriage with full sexual expression. Intimacy has several essential ingredients. First, there is the need for an established, personal identity. Standing alone is the required position that occurs between the separation from parents and the attachment to and connection with husband or wife. Erick Erickson made identity the developmental task of adolescence and intimacy the task of young adulthood. Identity is prior to intimacy. He stated that "oneness is prior to twoness."[1] You cannot borrow yourself from your partner, and you cannot find yourself in another. You can share yourself with another, but not find it.

One of my favorite pictures is an enlarged photograph of two sea gulls making a perfect landing on the seashore. The picture is special for two reasons. First, the photograph was taken by a minister friend, developed, enlarged, and presented to me as a gift. Second, it captures the beauty and joy of a couple as the two sea gulls land in perfect symmetry and harmony. In a marriage enrichment event, I shared the photograph with the couples and asked them to tell me what they saw. Some responses were "harmony," "working together," and "being at the same place at the same time." One wife captured it best when she said, "It reminds me that in marriage until you learn to fly alone, you cannot fly together." Intimacy is for persons who have learned or who are in process of learning to fly alone, to solo.

A second element of intimacy in marriage is that of friendship. Marital friendship is that interest in and care for another that wants and works for the highest good for the other. It is the presence shared between partners who invite each other to be open, honest, vulnerable, and transparent. Friendship is the response partners make to each other's invitation to be present in ways not offered to another because each stands in the partner's grace and not in his or her own merit.

Third, intimacy is trust. Trust is a given in marriage when couples have nurtured it in courtship. Once it is established, it is understood to be present and remains so until it is seriously broken. An example of trust is a little girl who is coaxed by her father to jump in his arms. She wants to trust, but she is hesitant because he is yet untested. With her father's persistent encouragement and as she becomes less hesitant, she reaches that point of trust, of utter abandonment, and she jumps. She is assured by the safe catch and her father's firm, strong arms. He invites again. Still slightly hesitant, she jumps and is safely caught. In time, the hesitancy is gone completely, and the child jumps into her father's arms with complete trust. The landing might not be as firm each time, or it might be somewhat different at times, but her trust is complete. What if, just one time, either by accident or on purpose, the father misses? The trust that was so complete is now gone and is hard-pressed to return to its original level. Trust can be rebuilt with more coaxing, more hesitance. It can recover. The difference now is that it must be earned by the father.

Intimacy in marriage is based on a trust between two partners who have passed the test so that alternately each can jump, knowing that the other will be there to catch.

Intimacy is also passion. It is at times so intense that it wants to consume the other. To be with each other and not to touch would be as frustrating as sitting before a luscious, favorite meal in a straight jacket.

Romance is the thoughtful, unpredictable side of intimacy. Romance is the many ways a couple creates to say how special they are to each other. It is a kind word, a thoughtful note, a surprise call, a task shared, a favorite dish, or a planned event. It is whatever each finds that says, "Of all the people in the world, you are most special to me."

Intimacy can be found in marriages where couples are committed to growth. Growth is the environment in which intimacy best flourishes. A marriage in which a couple is supportive of the personal growth of each other and the marriage is a relational marriage where intimacy is experienced and expressed.

Intimacy is time that is pregnant with meaning. It can be, and often is, devoid of activity but not of presence. Intimacy is two persons well established within themselves who are the best of friends, committed to changing and growing, who find the time to be thoughtful, and who can appropriately be passionately out of control.

Intimacy in marriage occurs in a relationship that is flexible, not rigid; creative, not boring; pioneering, not settling. It occurs in a relationship in which feelings are respected, appreciated, and shared.

Intimacy in a relational marriage is the best context in which sex is good and where sex is encouraged to approach its potential as a creative gift of God. Intimacy is necessary for good sex. Sex is the fullest expression of marital intimacy.

For couples to enjoy and to maintain a good sexual relationship, they need to be aware of several sexually related issues that tend to restrict or negate sex as an expression of intimacy. First, there are sexual inhibitions and learned behaviors that are brought into marriage from early childhood or adolescence. Two that seem to be more common are premature ejaculation for men and frigidity for women.

Physically and emotionally, husbands warm up, heat up, and finish up more quickly than wives. For husbands to finish up when wives are starting up is mutually frustrating. Some of the problem is related to the differences indigenous to maleness and femaleness. In other ways, the problem is related to learned behaviors. Beginning in early adolescence and continuing on through adolescence and early adulthood as boys are becoming men, they sometimes respond to their sexual arousal by masturbating. The combination, a physical given and a learned behavior, produces in males a much quicker sexual process that is not compatible with the much slower female process. In marriage, the sexual frustration and anger produced by this continuing disappointment for both often wedges the couple apart. The lack of intimacy in their sexual relationship slowly slips out and interferes with their intimacy in other areas.

A second sexual inhibition that is learned and nurtured in childhood and adolescence for girls is frigidity. Frigidity is the inability of women to free themselves from learned behavior and negative messages, that sex is viewed as duty rather than as a gift to be enjoyed and shared. The sources that produce such a negative view of sex are many. The strong media image of a sexy woman, even those who sell soaps and sodas, is a "perfect ten." The media message is that only "perfects" can be sexy and enjoy and share sex. Some women grow up feeling that men like certain body shapes or sizes, and they do not match up. They use clothes, the best they can, to camouflage what they perceive to be lacking, but the thought or idea of being totally exposed to another, even in marriage, is so stressful and frightening that intimacy is blocked.

Some wives grow up in families in which their fathers were distant and critical. They learned to relate to them in cautious, self-protecting kinds of ways. It is easy to transfer those feelings from father to husband. The fear of intimacy is misplaced by a functional, dutiful wife who is much more comfortable "doing for" husband than she is "being with" husband.

Another source of frigidity in wives is the negative messages about sex that they both see and hear as children from their parents. A functional marriage in which sex is primarily a physical act that adults do communicates a very incomplete and negative impression about sex. In such marriages, sex at its best is a need that is present; the need is periodically met by wives dutifully and indifferently. This impression, reinforced by a marital atmosphere that treats sex silently and suspiciously, is difficult to overcome. It frequently lives on from generation to generation.

A final source of frigidity for wives is the inability of parents to know how to teach their daughters about sex. Parents often find it difficult to teach that sex is a beautiful gift of God while at the same time to teach that it is the misuse of sex that is bad. While true for husbands as well, the message seems to be much stronger for wives.

The double standard that made girls bad and boys heroes for having sex is still around, though somewhat more muted. In order to protect their daughters from getting pregnant, the message by parents is so broad and hard that girls are taught to view sex cautiously, suspiciously, and often negatively. The truth that sex is good, but like all good gifts it can be abused, misused, and marked down, is often lost. Many parents, reinforced by the church have failed to separate out the good gift of sex from the bad fruits of sex, and they have chosen to emphasize the latter at the expense of the former. Sex to these parents is more of a sin than it is a gift. One of the results is frigidity.

Beth and Bill have been married for six years. Bill is a minister, and Beth works part-time outside the home. They are both very friendly and sociable with winsome personalities. They find meaning in their work and enjoy each other. They are compatible, and they appreciate and love each other. They have a serious sexual problem.

Beth grew up in a family where she received a very strong no message about her sexual self. Beth's mother had gotten pregnant before marriage and brought great embarrassment to her Southern, genteel family. Beth had heard this repeatedly as a child and as an adolescent. The no message was so strong that she stayed guarded throughout her adolescence and early adulthood. She met Bill in college, and they were married. The expectation was that marriage would easily and automatically lift the brake on sex, and Beth would be sexually free and available to her husband. Six years later Beth and Bill were in marital counseling, and she was finding it extremely difficult to exchange the premarital no to a marital yes.

The focused problem for Bill and Beth was a sexual one. There was another problem more silent and pervasive than the sexual problem. Protected by their mutual value systems in which sex was a marital privilege, Beth was free in their courtship to be loving and responsive to Bill. They both enjoyed and appreciated the freedom they felt to be open, vulnerable, close, and to feel intimate.

In marriage that soon changed. Beth was more quickly

aware of the change than Bill, and she worked hard to
keep her fears from Bill. Marriage had confirmed her permission to have sex, but it did not free her to desire sex,
initiate it, or enjoy it. A pregnancy, a child, being a part-
time student, having a part-time job—these all served to
keep her fears in check and to keep them unknown to
Bill. She slowly moved from a relational person to a more
functional wife and mother. The symptom revealing her
suppressed fear was the accusation Beth made that Bill
never touched her unless he wanted to have sex. His confrontation that she had become more and more disinterested in sex added to her fears, and she sought counseling
for herself. Bill joined her later for some marital therapy
where the sexual inhibitions from Beth's childhood were
shared and worked through.

Developmental inhibitions and learned behavior in
childhood and adolescence are often transported into
marriage and manifest themselves initially in the sexual
realm, but, eventually, they restrict or deny intimacy.
Some of these inhibitions and behaviors are superficial,
and they are cut away by marital love and care. Others
are deeply embedded and need to be surgically removed
with the help of a trained therapist. Then the couple is
free to enjoy the gifts of a relational marriage.

A second sexually related issue that restricts intimacy
in marriage is sexual discomfort or pain. It is unreasonable to think that intimacy in a marriage can be nurtured
and shared when one of its best and most complete expressions—sex—is going to be uncomfortable or painful.
The pain will certainly serve as a barrier. It will block
both the pleasure and the freedom to pursue it or respond
to it. Couples who are shy or timid or not knowledgeable
about sex will oftentimes tolerate and bear the pain as if
it is indigenous to the experience.

The pain is often tolerated or kept secret by the partner

experiencing the pain. Eventually it will manifest itself in various ways: the lack of sexual initiative on the part of the one who feels the pain, diminishing initiative on the part of the one without the pain but who senses reservation on the part of the partner, and rejection of the pain-free partner by the partner with the pain.

Most pain that is identified with sexual intercourse in marriage can be easily corrected by the couple. Continuing or periodical pain deserves the attention and expertise of a medical doctor so that its cause can be identified, treated, and corrected. Unless one is masochistic, anticipated pain during sexual intercourse is like a darkness that slowly pervades the entire marriage, denying intimacy.

Another foe of sexual intimacy is unresolved conflict. A couple cannot love and fight at the same time. A couple can deal with their anger appropriately, resolve it, and share and experience love again. The saying that "the only good part of fighting is making up" is partially true. When couples work at compromising differences, flushing out clogged systems, or dismantling barriers, the anger that appears and collects is defused and worked out. In place of the tension, the estrangement, and the coldness, there is harmony, friendship, and warmth. This is often a pregnant moment for intimacy. Sexual intimacy is a beautiful and appropriate way to express the joy in marriage of moving from lostness to foundness, from separateness to closeness, and from foe to friend. It is often after times of intentional conflict resolution that couples experience and share some of their best moments of intimacy.

Conflict left unresolved in a relational marriage affects intimacy in a number of ways. First, it separates sex from intimacy and makes of it a physical activity. Unresolved conflict does not diminish the need for sex; it does significantly limit the need for and expression of intimacy.

Second, unresolved conflict allows a couple to choose sexual abstinence. It is generally true that wives, more so than husbands, prefer that sex be an expression of intimacy. Thus, when the intimacy is denied by the unresolved conflict, wives are much less interested in sex. Our culture has supported a sexual myth that men cannot do without sex. In marriage, unresolved conflict that fosters division and separation frequently causes marital partners to divert their sexual energies into other acceptable activities and roles. They become more productive in their jobs, in their tasks at home, and in their hobbies or extracurricular activities. A second myth about marital sex is that only wives withhold sex as a way to control and punish. Since husbands are frequently passive aggressive with their anger, to become disinterested in sex or withhold sex is often a very heavy passive-aggressive clout.

Another effect that anger from unresolved conflict has on marital intimacy and sex is what could be called "marital rights." In marriage, anger mixed with sexual need and energy can be demanding, insensitive, using, punishing, and illegal. Husbands claim that their sexual needs in marriage should ensure them their conjugal rights. The need is a right within itself regardless of the state of the marital union. The wife can respond to this expected sexual right with an indifference expressing itself by either withholding sex or, if not sex, all except the bare necessity: her body.

Intimacy in a relational marriage requires the resolution of conflict so the separated, estranged relationship can return to togetherness, closeness, friendship, and companionship. It is basic to relational living that couples do not want to act close or be close when they are angry with each other. They are eager to resolve the conflict, to express the anger, and to be at one again.

A final sexually related agenda that affects a couple's intimacy is the absence of passion. Passion is the physiological arousal and intense desire to be united with another. It is highly motivational. It is often a primary reason why some couples, especially young couples, get married. Passion can get couples married; it alone will not keep couples married. It is one of the essentials for marriage, but it is not enough. Most couples begin with an adequate amount of passion, but the failure to nurture and grow the marriage can slowly or quickly destroy it. The powerful urge and need for sex which is present in courtship and early marriage is a strong motivational force in the desire to get married. In marriage, if passion is kept alive and well, it requires more than just the need for sex. Marriage assigns couples the double tasks of staying personally attractive to each other and growing a relationship that is attractive.

Passion does not live well in marriages that become predictable, boring, and dull. It does not survive well in marriages when couples cease to woo and court each other. Passion tends to fade in marriages where partners cease to give attention to their own growth; it fades where partners become undisciplined about their appearance, their manners and behavior, or their spiritual, emotional, and physical health. Passion is born of sex, but it thrives in a growing, changing, and dynamic relationship.

In relational marriages where intimacy is present and shared, sex is sometimes a functional act. It is unrealistic to expect sex to always be an expression of intimacy. There is a place for functional sex in a relational marriage. Fatigue is a common factor in marriage that often separates sex from intimacy. The sexual act requires both physical and emotional energy, and, if one or both are tired, they can share intimacy only if they claim their fatigue and agree to enjoy each other without sex. If they agree to have sex, it will be more functional than relational because the emotional and physical energy necessary for intimacy are not available. At this point they are relational in their openness with each other and functional in the act of sex.

Sex in marriage is not always accompanied by oohs and ahs, stars shooting off, and multiple climaxes. Neither is sex to always be a completion of intimacy. There is a place, and there are times in marriage when sex is an end within itself. Perfection is absent in all other areas of married life, and so it is in marital sex. In relational marriages, sex is occasionally functional. Every good meal does not end with a dessert. A slice of bread is often sufficient. The critical difference is that sex is not always functional.

A relational marriage by nature is solicitous of intimacy. The intention for intimacy is innate. Its expression can be impeded or sabotaged by physical fatigue that restricts or augments the emotions, by developmental sexual inhibitions that are suppressed but actively present, by unresolved conflict that builds a wall which separates, and by physical pain that diminishes sexual desires. When, for whatever reason, a relational marriage is without intimacy, the partners will actively engage themselves in seeking the help necessary to correct the problem, so they can share their "oneness" again. Sex for a relational couple is never enough. Intimacy is the gift they share with each other. Intimacy has the capacity to take sex and raise it to its fullest and best expression.

In a functional marriage, physical sex is usually all that a couple expects or shares. Usually, the pattern is

one in which a couple enters into marriage with a newness and passion that makes sexual expression exciting
and frequent. As the couple settles in to a marriage that
is no longer new, where passion has subsided, and where
roles and duties and functions are mutually assigned, sex
begins to lose some of its appeal. It is still valid yet less
frequent and exciting. It is said that, for some couples,
marriage has a way of "killing off" sex. The newness and
excitement of marriage are replaced by career changes
and demands. Marital novelty is replaced by parenting
roles and responsibilities or by volunteer and recreation-
al activities. The relational potential that was present in
the newness and excitement of early marriage has been
snuffed out by the functional tasks of marital and family
living. The functions are valid and necessary, but they
are no substitute for a relationship. As the relational potential is slowly dimmed and darkened, so is the expression of intimacy. To take its place is another marital function: sex.

This change from a relational position early in marriage to a functional style, later in marriage, can occur
simultaneously for the partners, or it can take place individually. Most couples experience the latter.

Marriages in which both partners are highly functional
in training and need are more accepting of sex as one of
those functional needs. They tend to extract from it its
gifts of power, pleasure, and production. Other couples
who are blends of varying degrees of relational and functional needs find sex to be a most frequent source of conflict. It is in this marital arena that both or one can come
with greater and different expectations. Even in functional marriages relational needs are present though
more dormant and suppressed. It is in the sexual area
that those relational needs are more evident.

Wives tend to become less and less interested in sex

when it is a marital duty or function. One reason for this is that functional sex tends to favor the husband in what it delivers. While taking care of his physical needs for pleasure and release, it often leaves the wife neither pleasured nor relieved. The husband, satisfied in terms of what he wants and expects, returns to sex frequently. The wife, frustrated and disappointed, is dutifully present but with less expectation and participation. Physical fatigue, preoccupation with wifely and motherly responsibilities, change in bedtime habits, and bodily ailments like headaches and stomach cramps are progressively more present to defend her against a marital right that leaves her so frustrated and disappointed. For a wife, duty has never been a strong motivation for sex, and the best it can do is meet the sexual needs of her husband. Duty, at best, over a period of time, provides the body necessary for sex. But that is all. When duty is the primary motivation for either sexual partner, they neither expect much from the act, nor do they actively participate in the act.

For the husband, the lack of involvement on the part of the wife bothers him but seldom stops him. Turning her on and drawing her into active participation with him has always been important, but seldom openly acknowledged and expressed. To do this would lean them in the direction of a relationship, and that would require far more change than just sex. Thus, sex in many marriages keeps on occurring, sometimes less frequently. For the husband there is no less pleasure, but for the wife, less participation.

Husbands, who in the past have been satisfied with functional sex, are now expecting more. A more open stance about sex and sexual expression in society has nurtured a higher expectation and, thus, a greater demand for sex to be more than a quick moment of physical pleasure and release. Husbands who are functional in their jobs and in their marriages expect things to be different in bed.

Husbands measure their sense of masculinity in two primary ways: achievement and sex. Achievement is a tangible, measurable expression of human need to produce, to create, and to provide. The business world builds into its system ways whereby men are rewarded for their creativity and ingenuity, for their loyalty and dedication, for their industry and production. Sometimes workers are presented a plaque or pin or gifts that recognize and appreciate achievement. Other times, it is a promotion that singles out a person's usefulness to the corporation, business, or institution. The most common and most appreciated expression of achievement in the job is a monetary raise. With the money, men are able to purchase and provide those things for themselves and their families that note success and support their need to be seen as masculine. Achievement, whether in the job or in sports, is critical to their feeling strong, independent, productive, and aggressive—all viewed in Western culture as masculine qualities.

A second measure of masculinity is sex. Husbands have traditionally viewed their sexuality as primarily related to their body image or to their ability to conquer. They measure their sexual prowess in terms of number of times. Such a view of masculinity propagates a functional approach to sex because it minimizes the need for a relationship. It uses sex as a tool to express power and to find pleasure. It disregards the need for intimacy that is present in mutual sharing. A traditional view of masculinity and functional sex have long been mutual friends.

A noticeable change has occurred with husbands in regard to how they measure their masculinity sexually. In the past it was number of times. Now it is more centered on what kind of lover he is, based on the responses he gets from his wife. Husbands have become so concerned with being "successful" lovers that they often fail to be relational partners.

Since husbands tend to measure their masculinity by success in the job and success in the bed, they often find themselves in a catch-22. In the job and in the marriage, being functional to them is the key to success. In the bed, success is primarily relational and secondarily functional. How can and does a husband turn down the functional self and turn up the relational self in bed? Or, if he can and does, how does the wife, who feels relationally ignored in the marriage, become relationally present in the bed? If a good sex life is dependent on a relational marriage—and I believe it is—then husbands are going to the bed expecting their masculinity to be affirmed, but they are finding their wives either functionally present, dutifully present, or angrily present. Instead of affirmation, husbands experience disappointment, frustration, rejection, and failure. Often their wives are blamed and accused of being asexual, frigid, or inhibited. They counter these accusations with direct anger or with behavior that is passive aggressive. A wife will say to her husband, "I cannot be responsive to you in bed when you are not interested in me in the den." Or a wife will respond to her husband's sexual interest and approaches with, "I don't feel well," or, "The children are up," or, "I have to finish these clothes." In order to be a good lover and thus a real man, a husband has to get his wife involved in the sexual experience. The husband is often unaware that her lack of involvement is not because of her disinterest, her inhibitions, or her preoccupation. It is because she is either unwilling or incapable of being switched on to relational in bed when he has been switched off to relational in the marriage.

A second noticeable change has occurred that impounds the marital relationship. It is that wives who have been programmed and assumed primary responsibility for the relational state of the marriage and family are now being programmed to be vocationally independent and successful. Dual career marriages represent a growing majority of marriages today. In the past, wives assumed primary responsibility to make the marriage and family relational. They were assigned that task early in life, as children, and they saw that task as high priority. Wives today still assume primary responsibility for marriage and family, but they accept it from a changed position. They come to marriage with a different program in which they view independence, vocational achievement, and marital equality to be personal, not sexual.

In moving out of the home place into the marketplace, several changes have occurred. One, wives can no longer be held solely accountable for marital and family relationships. That is to be mutually shared by both husband and wife. Secondly, wives who work in a functional setting find it more difficult to want and to keep the relational needs in marriage primary. Thus, husbands who come to marital sex with relational expectations are finding wives who are more satisfied with functional sex. Husbands and wives have slowly exchanged places.

The companionship style of marriage built on personal equity without functional equality—where relational needs are as valid as functional needs, and roles are defined by needs and not gender—is a biblical model of marriage that does not allow the changes in society affecting marriage and the family to cause couples to retreat back into a world of the past. Changes are new opportunities with new demands to make of marriage all that God meant it to be. New wine is not to be put into old wineskins. Couples who make new wine and put it in new wineskins keep their relationships primary. One of the joys of that new wine is sex, the best and fullest expression of marital intimacy.

Relational/Functional Exercise

Using the five-noted characteristics contrasting a relational and functional marriage, each marriage partner is to evaluate ther marriage as relational or functional. The scale is one to ten, ten being the maximum relational. Give first your own perception of how you see the marriage, and then give your perception of how your partner sees the marriage.

Functional   Relational

1	2	3	4	5	6	7	8	9	10
							h		w

1. Change Versus Sameness
2. Feelings Versus Facts
3. Conflict Resolution Versus
   Unresolved Conflict
4. Intimacy Versus Sex

Intimacy Versus Sex

1. Each marriage partner completes the following statements and then shares them with the other partner.

1. That which I most enjoy about our sex life is

_____

2. That which I would like to see us improve in our sex life is

_____

3. If you were going to ask me to do one thing that would enhance our sex life it would be

_____

4. The difference between sex and intimacy is

_____

5. The most essential element in a good sex life is

_____

2. You as a couple have just been handed a gift certificate in which you can spend an evening together to do whatever you wish. Money is plentiful; time is uninterrupted; the place is as near as your best imagination. How would you spend the evening? Free your playful child. Use your best imagination. Then share with each other how you would spend that evening.

Note

1. Erick Erickson, *Childhood and Society.*

8

Emotional Needs Versus Physical Needs

Marriage is a relationship in which value is shared, not borrowed.

Unmet needs in marriage are very much like a stone in your shoe. They cease to control the relationship when they are addressed directly.

In a society that is highly functional in nature, physical needs are primary, and emotional needs are secondary. Most of our time is spent assuring ourselves and our families that our basic needs—food, clothing, and shelter—are met. Abraham Maslow, out of his research with healthy persons, established physiological needs as the base for his pyramid of needs. These are our survival needs. They understandably take priority over other needs like safety, belonging, esteem, and self-actualization needs. It is a common agreement that a person who has no bread needs only bread.

Survival needs are primary, and we must have them met to live. These basic needs that seem so simple become very complex when survival needs and achievement needs become mixed. How much does one need to survive? That question is a simple one to poor people who have little or nothing. That same question becomes more complex as it is raised with couples who are working hard to overcompensate for a past in which extras were confined primarily to special occasions. To a couple who have just finished their educational goals, for whom money has been tight, physiological needs have been controlling and dominant; as they enter the professional work world, how much is necessary to physical and social survival? At this point neither the questions nor the answers are simple. Physiological needs are so interfaced with emotional needs that what is enough to survive at all the economic and social levels is relative.

In a functional society, things are the obvious test of success. What we eat, where we live, and what we wear are measurable expressions of who we are, where we are, whether or not we feel safe, if we belong, how we feel about ourselves, and if we are actualized. When success and survival needs mix, there is a sense in which enough is seldom enough. Meeting of physiological needs at a higher and greater level becomes not only the measurable standard by which we judge ourselves but the motivational force that urges and propels us to work and achieve. To seek to negate the need to achieve as measured by the basics—food, clothing, and shelter—or to address this need to achieve as if the need is negative or bad or unchristian is unfounded. To raise a couple's consciousness as to how they allow these more tangible, measurable, and physiological needs to dominate their marital lives and become a substitute for the more intangible needs within marriage is a worthy purpose. The thesis is that since our society is a highly functional one, and since couples spend so much of their time and energies in that arena, then couples need to intentionally will that their marriage and families are not extensions of that arena. Couples must intend that their relational needs which are emotional as well as physical are not neglected or overlooked.

If one's physiological needs are defined generally as food, clothing, and shelter, what are the emotional needs? Maslow identifies them as safety, belonging, esteem, and

self-actualization needs. Emotional needs are closely related to physical needs. They are separate from physical
needs in that they are present when the physical needs
are met, and they cannot be satisfied by physical substitutes. They can be identified as the need to feel special to
oneself, special to another, and special to others. Another
way to describe emotional needs is the need to feel valued
by oneself, by another, and by others.

I recall as a teenager that a pastor in a sermon said, "If
you were the only person in the world, Christ would have
died for you." It was not the theology of that statement
that got and kept my attention. It was the value that God
puts on a person. Since my adolescence, the biblical principle that has influenced my life and ministry most has
been the value God places on personhood. One of Jesus'
most popular parables, "The Prodigal Son," and two others less known and popular in that trilogy, "The Lost
Coin" and "The Lost Sheep," announce clearly and gladly
the value He and God place on the lost one (Luke 15). The
need to value and to be valued, the need to feel special
and to cause others to feel special, are as essential to our
health and wholeness as are our physiological needs.

In marriage, emotional needs are those needs each
partner has to feel and to share his or her value as a person with the marital partner. Those needs take various
forms and shapes such as the need to belong to another, to
feel safe and secure with the other, to be respected and
appreciated by the other, to know that their loyalty and
devotion to each other is unlike that to any other, to continue to be seen and related to as attractive, to be treated
as a person of equal value and importance, to be treated
with kindness, to be accepted and have that acceptance
grounded in grace, not merit, and to be seen as a winner
even in the midst of failure and disappointment.

Mary is a young woman in her early twenties who came

to counseling to work through the lodged negative feelings about herself augmented by a divorce. Mary, like most, had approached and entered marriage as a permanent commitment. The fact that her marriage had ended after two years made divorce almost unbearable. She was dealing with the grief from losing her marriage and her marital status. She was also dealing with feeling that the quickness of her divorce called into question her ability to make good decisions which was something she had sought to do as a young person and adult. For making good decisions she had received personal affirmations from several significant adults in her life. Now she was having to admit to herself and others that her marriage had been a bad decision. After some six months in counseling, working through her grief, she stated, "I can now look back on my divorce and see that a bad thing happened to me. But I am not a bad person."

Emotional needs in marriage are addressed in several ways. First there is the personal and marital assurance that is nurtured by the strength, security, and stability of the marital state. The bumps and bruises that are part and parcel of marriage itself are not threatening to the commitment that was made and remade daily to both marriage and each other. The thought of divorce that sometimes is a companion to marital bumps and bruises is no more than a thought. It appears and disappears and leaves no lingering debris. Safety and belonging needs are intact and met. Secondly, there is a personal and marital reassurance growing out of developing a dependable pattern of taking the separation that results from differences and disagreements and working it through so that there is restitution and recovery. Marital reality accepts separation as a given. Learning how to address emotional estrangement so that it does not have to be feared, ignored, or endured—but rather handled creatively—

builds a marital pattern that is dependable, one that can be trusted. Thus, in the presence of conflict couples do not have to build and maintain protective bastions, but they can fight fairly out in the open. Thirdly, emotional needs are met when marital partners are creatively sensitive to each other's needs to feel valued and find opportunities to express that sensitivity in surprising and unexpected ways.

Special days and occasions are calendared opportunities for couples to express their appreciation and love for each other, but they are limited in their power to bless. A hug (a word, a note, a touch) that is not calendared or expected, that is not for the purpose of making up, that is an end and not a means, has an unlimited power to bless. Emotional needs are present and real. Relational marriages are aware of them and seek out ways to meet them.

Since emotional needs are so closely related to one's feeling valued, it is important that one understand that value is not earned or borrowed. It is accepted and shared. From a Christian perspective, personal value is not earned by our goodness. It is God's gift to us to be accepted. For anyone who seeks to base value on goodness, one somehow is never good enough. Goodness is an expression of value, not a means to achieve it. Our value rests in God's goodness and not in our own. Our value is His gift. We only need to accept it and let the gift work within us both the desire to be good and the expressions of doing good. Our value is grounded in creation and re-creation, both acts of God.

Marriage is a relationship in which value is shared. It is not earned or borrowed. When marital partners look to the other for their value, they also expect the other to take responsibility for and to meet all their emotional needs. How one perceives and handles one's emotional needs is intricately woven into how one values oneself and where one looks for one's value.

The biblical revelation is clear that the value of a person is primary. God starts with persons and builds a family, a church, and a people. Each collection derives its strength and purpose from the value of one. The individual is both the foundation for all relationships and the creation of relationships. There is no person apart from community. No person is one unto himself or herself. Thus one's identity is who one is developmentally, biologically, socially, emotionally, and spiritually.

Influence is a biblical theme that is treated seriously. A biblical mandate to deal wisely with influence is given by Christ when He said to His disciples, "Whoever receives one such child in my name receives me; but whoever causes one of these little ones who believe in me to sin, it would be better for him to have a great millstone fastened round his neck and to be drowned in the depth of the sea" (Matt. 18:5-6). Individuals are like clay in the potter's hand. Each one is to be influenced, touched, and shaped by many potters whose only task is to produce the form for which the clay was made. Each of us is the product of all that is uniquely ours—past, present, and future— somehow meeting to form a person, an individual of supreme value.

At the same time, relationship at any level rests on the foundation of individuals. It is true that the strength of a chain is as strong as its weakest link. The individual is the foundation for all relationships. Relationships are as hearty and strong as are the persons in them. Just as healthy individuals are produced by healthy relationships, healthy relationships are produced by healthy persons. To use Paul's analogy, the eye is not the body; it is only a part of the body. Yet the health of the part is critical to the health of the body. The part is one on a team,

and the team is the result of the parts: each valid, each
strong, each good (1 Cor. 12:14 *ff.*). One is created by
many, and the many rest on the one as illustrated by the
following diagram:

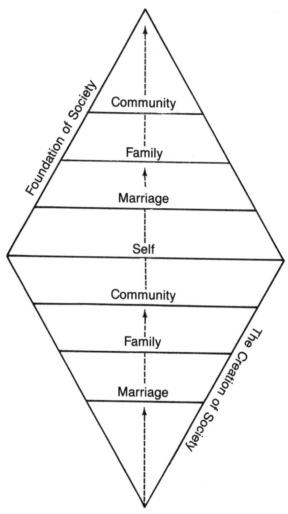

Karen has been in personal therapy for a year. During

that period of time, her husband joined her as they sought to work through a crisis related to her extramarital involvement. The marital therapy was able to defuse the intensity level created by the affair, specifically, and the more general disappointment produced by the strained marriage. The husband, less needful to hurt and to punish but still very much unfinished with the wife's behavior, chose to opt out of the marital therapy. The wife continued in therapy where the primary focus was on her need to establish her own value. She needed to find her own place in the world where she could feel positive and productive. She had entered marriage with a man she loved, but also with a man who she unconsciously thought could give her value and fill her life with meaning and purpose. He had not been sufficiently able to do either. Then she blamed him for her unhappiness. Out of her marital disappointment and anger, and with her unmet emotional need for affection and attention, she had sought to disregard her value system and find her value as a person from someone else.

Marriage is not a relationship that is capable of handling and taking care of excessive emotional needs founded in unfinished childhood and adolescent development. Marriage, like different types of electrical wiring, can handle only so much emotional current. Too much current or the wear and tear at maximum capacity over an extended period of time can cause the fuse to blow. Trying to extract from marriage more than marriage can handle is one of the more common marital problems. It manifests itself in more obvious and familiar symptoms like extramarital affairs, workaholics, frigidity, depression, parenting overkill, church and community involvement.

There are some observed patterns that are socially produced and reinforced as to how wives and husbands perceive their emotional needs, and how they react to those needs not being met or to their excessive demands. There are some general patterns that have frequent exceptions.

First, some general observations about wives. Wives still assume and take primary responsibility for the marital relationship. Relationships in our culture have been placed under the care and keeping of women. In a society that is keyed on production, relationships are downplayed, and functions are magnified. Functions belong to both, but relationships belong primarily to women. Too, since production is a masculine line, functions are viewed as positive and critical. Relationships are a feminine line and are often viewed as less important and nonessential.

Second, because women are identified with relational needs, they are often viewed and related to as a weaker, more fickle, and emotional sex. To accept this generalized assumption is profitable to both men and women. It feeds the exaggerated egos of men who need to be in charge, to feel strong and masculine. For women, it allows them to be irresponsible for their own personal welfare and to depend on someone else for their value and welfare. Freedom, for some wives, is found in not having to punch the clock or in not having to live by someone else's prescribed schedule. Often, these selfish needs and benefits are supported by the biblical prescription that women are born to be submissive, dependent, and second class. Chosen submission is a biblical principle that is not sexually prescribed or reinforced. A wife's interest in and concern for relational living is not born from weakness. It is born from strength. It is not feminine or masculine. It is of God.

Third, wives are more aware of and open about their emotional needs. Relationships, to remain vibrant and healthy, must share emotional needs. Wives are more in tune to those needs. If the relationship is strained temporarily or permanently blocked, wives take the initiative more often than husbands to confront the anger and resentment created by unmet emotional needs. Wives also place a higher priority on emotional needs and seek to meet the emotional needs of their husbands in consistent and spontaneous ways. A father in counseling, who was painfully concerned about the failure of his son's marriage, said, "Ann did not see the need to be supportive of Tom in a way that made him feel good about himself and his work." The father had received an ample amount of that kind of support from his wife, and he saw it as essential to a good marriage. The father had observed something missing in his son's marriage. Tom was much more sensitive to and involved in meeting his wife's emotional needs. The more obvious insight was: the father saw the wife's need to be in tune to his son's emotional needs as a given that comes with being a woman and with the role of wife. Wives are more comfortable with emotional needs than husbands, and society expects that. In a relational marriage, both partners are sensitive to emotional needs and are open with each other in both expressing those needs and meeting them.

As noted in an earlier chapter, if one partner is relational and the other is functional, the marriage will either slowly or quickly move toward being divided or toward being functional. One partner cannot take an open position toward expressing emotional needs and continue that way alone. The consistency of being emotionally closed and disinterested on the part of the functional partner will cause the relational partner to shut down and become more and more functional, or give expression to anger in some rather expected and predictable ways.

There is a noticeable trend in regard to wives and emotional needs that is worth noting. As women enter and work in the job market where functions are paramount and production and competition are expected, they are prone to a desensitization of emotional needs and of sharing them. Thus marriages that began relationally become functional more quickly as both give up the need to make emotional needs valuable. This, in no way, supports the often-given blanket solutions to marital problems: if wives would "stay where they belong" or if persons have prescribed places in the home, marriages would somehow automatically get well, and the divorce rate would decline substantially. That was the same argument that was used in the Deep South about racial unrest. The thinking seems to be that certain people—races, sexes— have assigned places—created by social systems (often assigned to God)—and, if everyone would find their place, get in it, and be satisfied with it, all would be well. This thinking needs to be resisted and confronted wherever it is found. More and more wives in the work force cause some changes in marriage and families that verbalized equality will not remedy. A demonstrated equality where there is a partnership—both partners are intentional about their emotional needs and their responsibility to share them, address them, and appropriately meet them—is the task of marriage today, and it must be mutually shared. Research suggests husbands agree that if both wife and husband work outside the home, the home responsibilities are to be shared equally down the middle. Husbands agree in principle and then act differently, still expecting the wife to be primary homemaker and keeper. Husbands give assent in the same way to the meeting of emotional needs and then act to the contrary, leaving the primary task of emotional "making and keeping" to the wife. In both tasks, the wife often becomes frustrated and angry, and she acts out that anger in inappropriate ways. The wife working outside the home effects change in many ways: two obvious ones are the desensitization to emotional needs in marriage by the wife and the unwillingness by her to assume single responsibility for those emotional needs.

Another factor present in the dual career marriages is that of time. The requirements of the job and the home and family responsibilities compete for time. Time for the emotional needs of the marriage has to be prioritized because there are many good and worthwhile family and community needs that compete for time. To schedule a time for emotional needs does not demean either the need or the specialness of the relationship. To schedule time, or to ask for time, may not match up to a romantic, untested perception of marriage, but it does take care of the marriage.

Another issue present in dual career marriages is that of energy. When two persons come home tired, the potential for disappointment and disagreement is doubled. As one wife stated, "I found myself not interested in my husband's emotional needs because that takes energy, and there was none left."

This lack of energy is not an energy just for dual career marriages. The more traditional marriage, where the husband's career is outside the home and the wife's inside the home, often has the same energy issue. Whether two work outside the home—or one does, and the other does not—the necessary energy to meet emotional needs is a critical factor. Dual career marriages have the same responsibilities for meeting the emotional needs of each other and the family. When those needs are equally understood, equally considered and addressed by both partners, and the weight of the physical and emotional needs of the marriage is shared, the marriage is freed from chronic anger and resentment either suppressed or expressed in inappropriate ways. Shared responsibility for the couple's emotional needs makes for a healthy marriage. Good marriages energize the partners so that there is enough energy present for the task of meeting the emotional needs. Research and experience teaches us that healthy marriages energize, and unhealthy marriages de-energize.

The key to relational marriages is intentionality. Romantic energy is a definite asset, but it is not enough to carry the marriage on a day-to-day basis and over a life-long commitment and course. The will to do and to grow and to love, infused by romantic energy, is necessary for meeting the emotional needs of marriage. Thus, whether the marriage is more traditional—husband's work is outside the home and the wife's inside the home—or more contemporary—dual career marriages—the pace and demands of life require that couples enter into marriage more intentional and stay in marriage with a will to love and care for each other's emotional needs.

Now some general observations about husbands: husbands, if not verbally, behaviorally still assume that the relational needs of marriage rest primarily with wives. The social program and context is changing, but its historical influence is still present. Husbands are becoming more sensitive to the mutual marital responsibility for emotional needs. The natural working out of that sensitivity is still impeded by family and societal programming that has been forceful in shaping the masculine mind and his established and perceived roles. Without an intention that works to reshape and redirect their masculine minds, husbands still tend to leave the primary care of emotional needs to wives. They go at it in spurts often as a response to a situation such as a wife's illness or because of the dramatic confrontation of an angry wife, or after some redemptive guilt produced by a sermon, a book, or a marriage enrichment event. The intention is genuine but short-lived.

Sam and Marcia have been married for eighteen years. She is a homemaker, and he is a respected, successful accountant. For fourteen years they lived well with a marital partnership in which she carried the emotional needs of the marriage and family, and he carried the physiological needs. Into the fifteenth year what had seemed to work well began to show symptoms of unrest and emotional fatigue and burnout. Marcia, at first, asked for more involvement on his part in meeting the emotional needs of the marriage and family. Sensing a deaf ear to her frequent requests, she next demanded more involvement on Sam's part. Her demand for help and his need to maintain the status quo produced more and more open conflict and fighting. Next she became depressed and underwent surgery for some physical problems that were not created by the marital stress but were greatly exaggerated by it. The next step was marital counseling. The mounting history of marital unhappiness, the need for change by her, and the need for status quo by him had nurtured a strong, thick wall of resentment. After eight months of counseling, the positions remained intact and separation and divorce became a real option. Trying to utilize the remaining benefits, their common marital and family commitment, a three months time frame was contracted and agreed on in which they would try to nurture back and reroute their marriage. As part of the contract, the husband agreed to assume primary responsibility for their emotional needs. Marcia, as a way of self-preservation, had become cold and numb toward Sam. Marcia said to Sam as they talked about the contract: "I am not yet stone, but ice. A consistent effort on your part to be sensitive to our emotional needs, and to demonstrate a change of mind in terms of your responsibility for our emotional welfare, can slowly change the ice to a warm, sharing person again."

The apparent benefits produced in Sam a genuine spurt of interest and concern. His family history of clearly defined masculine roles, his social program that had confirmed those roles, and fourteen years of unchallenged history of those roles in marriage had produced in him a mind-set that could hear the truth, but not do the truth. It was necessary that he do the truth, so he could be freed from his personal confinement and they from their marital stress.

There are some Christian counselors and Christians who clearly see that the resolution to this most common marital vignette is submission on the part of the wife (Eph. 5:22-24). A mutual submission in which both husbands and wives assume equal responsibility for the emotional needs of the marriage makes a much more fair and healthy context: submission by each or by either is a chosen expression of love and not a prescribed duty of law. (Ephesians 5:21 keeps 5:22-24,25-30 from being used to support a power play for personal or sexual domination.) In a relational marriage, the responsibility for meeting the emotional needs of the marriage is equally shared and demonstrated.

A second general observation about husbands is what may be called the "Sampson Syndrome." Emotional vulnerability, for men, is to be avoided. The fear that husbands have of being controlled, dominated, or used by wives has several sources. *Henpecked* is the label of the past, and *submissive* is the more present one. The labels change, but the feeling remains the same. A man who is controlled by a woman is no man.

Another source that nurtures the fear is the developmental task of individuating, the separating of oneself from parents. A significant change occurs when Jim becomes Jim Smith rather than Jim Smith, the son of Mr. and Mrs. Harold Smith. There are some peculiar aspects of this process that relate to the parent of the opposite sex. Whether the peculiarity comes from the child's sexual attraction to the parent of the opposite sex—the Oedipus complex—or from the son's need to test out his developing masculine skills with the opposite sex, or the need to be more private and independent with his feelings and thoughts, the son needs to get emotional space. The adolescent, in order to feel manly, often swings far away because excess is the only felt resolution for his need to separate and space himself from his parents. In childhood and early adolescence there was mutual sharing between mother and son. Now she gets no more than one word answers or even grunts to her questions. If excess emotional distance is the way to get space from one woman, then, at a feeling level, it is the way to get and keep space from all women. Not just space, but too much space, becomes a masculine coping mechanism that keeps a man from being controlled and, at the same time, emotionally detached from the needs of his wife. What often protects him can also strangle him.

Soon after we were married, I became aware of some angry feelings toward my wife when she would call the office occasionally and ask me to stop by the store and get some milk or bread. Her requests were certainly appropriate and infrequent, but my feelings of anger precipitated by her requests were not. It was years later that I was able to connect my present feelings to my childhood experience in which my perfectionistic mother made frequent requests of me to do jobs and chores for her.

My mother's obsession with cleanliness was unmatched. Her obsession plus nine children equaled an impossible task. Since Mother was unable or unwilling to

live with less than perfection, I, the seventh child, got sin-
gled out as Mother's junior partner in her call to have and
keep the cleanest house in the county. At a feeling level, I
still believe "cleanliness is next to godliness" to be a biblical mandate.

My mother had an eye for the most minute imperfec-
tion, and she certainly called out orders to her junior offi-
cer. "Get the broom and sweep off the porch," or, "See
that string over there," or, "Get that piece of paper by the
road," or, "Pull that weed," or, "Pick up that towel."
When I got old enough to figure out a plan that would
work, I got my space because I felt space was the only way
to get a military leave of absence from my mom.

My mom was afraid of water and constantly warned us
about its harmful nature. We had a six-acre pond in front
of our house, a good 500 yards away. Aware that my
mother was afraid of water, my plan for escape was to go
to the pond, get in the fishing boat, push out from the
bank, and float—undisturbed—for hours while she frequently called, "Bob, Bob, come here right now!"

The request by my wife to stop by the store and get a
loaf of bread had connected with those stored memories
in my childhood. Instead of an adult-to adult-response, I
had reacted out of my childhood to my mother's unrelent-
ing requests. Instead of retreating to the pond where I got
my physical space from my mom, I was using inappropriate anger to get emotional space from my wife. As an
adult I was acting as if running or fighting were the only
options available to get needed space. As a child, the option to claim it was not mine. As an adult, with an understanding adult, it was.

The distancing behavior men choose, or were forced to
choose with their mothers, is the same behavior they often use with their wives. In marriage, men need to make
two distinctions: one, they are not children, and, two,

they are not married to their moms. Adults know how to ask for space and give space. To be close, to be emotionally vulnerable, is not the same as being controlled.

A third general observation about husbands is that husbands need and want relational wives. Generally speaking, wives are more relational than men; men appreciate and enjoy that. Wives' more natural, open approach to emotional needs is seldom unappreciated by their husbands, but it is often not reciprocated. This creates a situation in which one (the wife usually) must take full or primary responsibility for meeting the emotional needs of the other, adjust to the nonmeeting of emotional needs by both, become increasingly frustrated and angry, feel trapped in a closed system, or seek relief through divorce. All the options present in a one-way emotional, need-meeting marriage—the wife assuming and carrying the full load (emotional burnout), the frustration created by unmet needs (anger), and finding a way out (divorce)—produce behavior on the part of the wife that is used by the husband to support his functional position in marriage. The resulting behavior can also cause the wife to be blamed for the growing separation and conflict in the marriage.

The other option, the wife choosing to become functional herself in order to be more compatible with her functional husband, produces some observable patterns. First, if the conflict created by the relational/functional marriage has been present but not confronted, the husband can feel a sense of relief and he can remain functional in a more relaxed way. The wife's choice to be functional takes some pressure off the husband. Secondly, the husband can feel a sense of loss in that one of the initial and continuing attractions, his wife's relational person and personality, is fading or significantly different. Comments like "What's going on with you?" or, "Where is your warmth and vitality?" or, "You are becoming something I don't like" are frequently made. What was special about her is muted or gone. Even though the husband misses it, he is still unaware of how he relates to her change; or, if he is aware of it, he is not yet ready or willing to make the changes within himself that nurture the relational within her. A third result is that relational sex has now become functional sex. Men who choose to be functional in all other aspects of their lives tend to be highly dissatisfied with functional sex. They prefer that life in the bedroom be responsive and satisfying.

A fourth observation is that in marriages where the husband's career-job is outside the home, and the wife's career is the home, the husband gets his emotional needs met from two primary sources: work and home. The wife has a sole primary source: home. The career/job world has much more defined ways to express the value of persons to their vocational family unit and system than does the home unit or system. Promotions, bonuses, plaques, trips, recognitions, and benefits are all very specific, measurable ways to recognize a person for good, productive work. Contrasted to that is the home career where good results depend equally upon hard work, good management, personal skills, and creativity. The appreciation for the job is often felt by the recipients but frequently unspoken or unrecognized in specific measurable ways. Since the emotional need to be appreciated and valued belongs to each, the wife often feels ignored, unappreciated, and taken for granted. The resulting behaviors seldom gravely affect her functional roles; they may often enhance them. Her desire and ability to accept and carry the relational needs of the marriage usually ebb or can diminish and frequently cease.

Recognition and appreciation are emotional needs in which the continuing ability to meet them in another is conversely related to having them met for oneself. Met emotional needs in marriage are the inexhaustible source that feeds and supports a growing relationship. The failure to meet the need of either adversely affects the life of both. In marriage there cannot be a giver and a receiver. There have to be two givers and two receivers.

Meeting Emotional Needs: A Plan

Partners in a marriage bring different need levels with different needs. The commonality of our humanness means that we all share the same needs. The difference that produces the conflict is that of need level. A list of common needs would include the following:

space
togetherness
intimacy
support
respect and appreciation for who I am
respect and appreciation for what I do
personal growth
marital growth
vocational growth
play
trust
affection
sharing
forgiveness
community
extended family
achievement
romance
touching

The needs are present in our humanness. They come

with being born. The level of need that couples bring to marriage is a result of our gathered life experiences: negative and positive. For example, Joan grew up in a family that enjoyed playing together. Family outings, games, and vacations were special times for her. Jim grew up in a family where play was allowed only after all work was completed or at very specific times like Saturday afternoons and holidays. Joan and Jim came to their marriage with both the need to work and the need to play. Jim, strongly motivated to achieve through hard work, eager to provide sufficiently for his family, and highly influenced by his family's work ethic, found less and less time to play. Joan missed the refreshment of play that had been present in her family and the home that it had produced. She sought, in both direct and indirect ways, to get Jim to join her in their need to play. It was not the total absence of play that was the issue. The issue was: Joan needed more play than Jim, and her unmet need for playtime with him was met with increasing resistance.

Bob grew up in a touching family. Hugs from his father and mother were frequent and natural. If family members felt close they showed it by touching. Betty grew up in a family where closeness was understood as a given by the family structure, but it was infrequently spoken or physically shown. In their marriage, touching was present, but Betty lived with the steady pressure produced by Bob's unspoken expectation for more.

One of the keys to marriage is the recognition, desire, and skill a couple have in mediating and compromising their different levels of emotional needs. The very uniqueness of the individuals recognized and affirmed as the gift each brings to the marital relationship is the origin of differences in emotional needs that is a primary source of stress and conflict. What a couple does with their differing need levels is a good indication of their relational health.

The first step in working out the difference is to identify those emotional needs where the differences are great enough to cause consistent irritation and conflict. One of the critical mistakes that couples make is: they convince themselves that the differences and their effects are temporary in nature and, with time, will disappear. A difference in emotional needs is very much like a small stone in one's shoe. One can keep walking expecting it to shift to the side. One can shift one's weight to the toes or to the heel of the foot, or, one can stop walking. To go on, one will need to address the stone directly. One will need to take the time to take off the shoe and remove the stone. The relief and the freedom to get on where you are going is always worth the time and effort it took to remove the stone. Unmet emotional needs in marriage are very much like that stone. They cease to control the relationship when they are addressed directly. The second step in mediating differences in emotional needs is to view compromise as a valid friend, not a malevolent foe. A compromise in marriage is like pouring water in a container that has two outlets. Whatever water is poured in pours out equally in both directions. Whenever two persons compromise a difference in marriage, the benefits that result from the strengthened relationship are shared mutually by each partner. If compromise is viewed by either partner as losing or giving in, it becomes a foe, and the negative results, too, are shared mutually by each partner. Compromise works because it takes away the impossible tasks and makes of them a workable reality.

Nan and Bill have been married for three years. Nan's need for affection and focused attention felt excessive to and demanding of Bill. Bill's need for much less affection and closeness felt like distance and insensitivity to Nan.

Attempts on Nan's part to get Bill more involved with her were met with humor and statements like: "Hey, we're married now," or, with what felt like to her, more and more distance. This agenda was verbalized by Nan in the first counseling session, but it was not pursued. It was filed away. After several sessions in which some trust was established, and some marital history was collected, I shared with them that one of the primary sources of conflict in the marriage was unmet needs. Nan's unmet need for focused attention and affection from Bill was seen by Bill as unreal. It was perceived as unreal by him for two reasons. First, his need level for affection was much less than hers. Secondly, the absence of enough affection for Nan had created a need for more. Nan was on the offensive, and Bill was on the defensive. The more she worked to get her need met, the harder he worked to keep from being engulfed. To radically alter their need level for affection seemed like an unworkable plan. Nan felt like she had fought for a right and had lost. Bill felt like Nan was unreasonable in her need for affection and felt justified in his giving even less. Nan was frustrated and angry, and her anger had been bottled and misplaced. Bill saw her as more distant and functional.

Significant change for any person is a slow process. Quick change is usually short-term. The initial response to significant change is one of resistance: "a digging in," a fortified position. Bill and Nan had dug in, and the marital relationship was the wounded, suffering casualty.

After the difference had been identified, I asked them to join me in a simple exercise. I drew a vertical line on the board and asked them to separately (so as not to be influenced by the other) respond to the following questions. On a scale of from zero to one hundred pounds, zero being minimum and one hundred being maximum, how many pounds of affection do you perceive the other needs, and how much do you need?

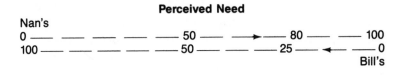

Perceived Need

Nan's
0 —— —— —— —— —— 50 —— ——▶—— 80 —— —— 100
100 —— —— —— —— —— 50 —— —— —— 25 —— ◀—— —— 0
Bill's

Actual Need

Nan's
0 —— ——▶—— —— —— 50 —— 60 —— —— —— —— 100
100 —— —— —— —— —— 50 —— —— —— 25 —— ◀—— —— 0
Bill's

Bill's perception of Nan's need is one of high need: eighty pounds, and Nan's perception of Bill's need is a low need: twenty-five pounds. Nan's assessment of her real need is lower but still on the elevated side. Bill's real need is consistent with Nan's perception of his need. Anytime there is a difference in need level greater than twenty pounds, there is a source of conflict present in the marriage that cannot be ignored. The marital stone has to be addressed directly, or it will create marital stress, pain, and estrangement.

Bill's need level for affection is twenty-five pounds. At the lowest, Nan's is sixty pounds. There is a thirty-five-pound need level difference. The maximum difference that can be tolerated and integrated into a marital relationship is a twenty-pound difference. In this case, each fort is set and fixed and continuously fortified by the occupant. For Nan to join Bill at his need level would be to give up something of herself. Her option is to turn elsewhere, primarily to their infant child. For Bill, to move to

Nan's need level he would have to become something other than himself. His option is to become more functional in the marriage and more productive in his job.

Compromise of the need-level difference is both essential and appropriate. Compromise in marriage is not stubbornly giving in. It is the willingness of both partners to move toward the middle as a way to resolve a difference and enrich the marriage. If Bill wills, not just desires, to increase his poundage from twenty-five to forty pounds, and Nan wills to lower her need level to fifty pounds, the mutual compromise has taken a conflict-producing situation and made it into a mutually satisfying one. Bill works on giving more, and Nan works on needing less. The result is a compromise that places the need at a level that is both mutually satisfying and realistically maintained. By compromising the need level, they meet the need.

Mike and Mary have been married for seven years. There has been a growing awareness that their need level for sex is different. The newness of the marriage and the dutiful response on Mary's part had kept the growing awareness disguised. Mary felt that Mike was oversexed, but she had no source or standard to confirm it. Mike felt Mary was somewhat frigid and, at least, disinterested in sex. Mike's sexual need, fed by his need to produce a more willing partner, increased his need for sex. Mary, feeling more uncomfortable and often feeling used or controlled by Mike's sexual needs, reacted with more sexual aloofness and suspicion. In reaction to each other, they were increasing their sexual need-level differences. He became more sexually demanding, and she became more sexually unavailable.

After several sessions in counseling, collecting a marital history that provided a context to understand and address their specific conflict-producing issues, I used with them the need-meeting exercise. I asked both of them to assign poundage to their perception of the other's sexual need and to their actual sexual need level.

Sexual perceived need level

Mary's
0 —— —— ——►25 —— —— ——►50 —— —— —— —— ——►100
100◄—— —— 80◄—— —— ——50◄—— —— —— —— —— —— 0
                                                    Mike's

Actual Sexual Need

Mary's
0 —— —— —— ——►40 ——►50 —— —— —— —— ——►100
100◄—— —— —— —— 65◄—— 50◄—— —— —— —— —— 0
                                                    Mike's

The actual need level differs only twenty-five pounds, five pounds over the workable level, but even there the need difference is great enough to be consistently conflict producing in the marriage, and the difference—like the stone in the shoe—cannot be ignored for long.

The perceived-need level difference is fifty-five pounds. Their perception grew out of frustrations produced by the unaddressed real need-level differences and the pursuing positions that were taken indicating "I am right, and you are wrong."

In their particular case, Mike moved almost completely away from a sexual relationship with Mary, channeling his sexual energies into work and meeting his sexual need by masturbating. Even though Mary's need level for sex was lower than Mike's, his move toward occasional sex caused her to feel rejected and suspicious.

After tapping into the accumulated anger, helping them to express it appropriately, I asked them to assess their sexual need level and consider a compromise. Mary's willingness to increase her sexual interest five pounds and Mike's willingness to decrease his ten pounds would bring them to a mutually acceptable position where their sexual needs were appreciated and met.

Change on the part of one to accommodate the other's need level is usually temporary in nature, accompanied by dutiful resentment, and thus disappointing to both. In marriage, when the difference in the need level is significant (twenty or more pounds), the resolution to the conflict produced by the difference is marital compromise. In the compromise, the good of the marriage takes precedence over the needs of the individuals. In return, giving priority to the marriage meets the needs of the individuals.

Meeting emotional needs in marriage is critical. In days past when life focused primarily around physical and functional needs, emotional needs were present but not viewed as critical to life or to marriage as were the more basic physical needs. As noted by Maslow's pyramid of needs, physical needs are dictatorial and critical where they are unmet. Even in marriage, when the basic needs are met, couples often establish the need level for more basic needs at such a high level that they make them and keep them central.

Dan and Donna both grew up in families that were functional and viewed by them as stable and secure. In counseling, they recalled their first few years of marriage as happy, stable, and secure. When asked to identify when the marital situation changed, they both almost in unison verbalized the day, month, and year. There was a loss of job, a birth of a child, a return to her family nest, a part-time job for her, and a new job for him that was stopgap and temporary. The result of all of this was a stress level that had taken its toll on each of them personally and on their marriage.

In counseling, it became obvious that the stress produced by the "crisis time" had left some marks on them personally and maritally. The marriage was in serious trouble. They separated and contemplated divorce, not from the stress, but from Dan's obsessive need to recover the security and stability he had grown up with in his family, and the stability they had known in the early years of their marriage. That, too, is noteworthy and understandable, but four years later, when things had stabilized, Dan remained obsessive. His primary need and concern was that what had happened once would not happen again. He became married to his work, and he gave himself almost totally to providing for their physical needs. His need for physical security was so strong that he transferred his need to Donna and strongly insisted that she become as intentional about a career as he. His insistence that she find "meaning for her life" in a job was obviously present for several reasons. First, the guilt he felt for spending unreasonable hours at work and the tension that it produced in the marriage would be somewhat appeased. Second, it would meet some of her emotional needs and relieve him of the responsibility of meeting them. Third, it would take some of the pressure off of him for being solely responsible for their physical security and stability. Fourth, it would support Dan's preferred marital stance: a functional one.

Dan's physical needs and Donna's emotional needs became active opponents. The result was a battered marriage that was in the early rounds but going for a predictable knockout. The earlier crisis of job loss had brought Dan and Donna back to the first level of Maslow's pyramid, and, for Dan, it had kept him there. Physical needs in a marriage cannot be measured by some imposed standard from without. Each marriage must define for itself what is enough. Enough is known and experienced within a marriage when physical needs share common ground with emotional needs so that, instead of being opponents, they are friends.

Relational/Functional Exercise

Using the five-noted characteristics contrasting a relational and functional marriage, each marriage partner is to evaluate the marriage as relational or functional. The scale is one to ten, ten being the maximum relational. Give first your own perception of how you see the marriage, and then give your perception of how your partner sees the marriage.

Functional   Relational

1	2	3	4	5	6	7	8	9	10
							h	w	

1. Change Versus Sameness
2. Communication: Feelings Versus Facts
3. Conflict Resolution Versus Unresolved Conflict
4. Intimacy Versus Sex
5. Emotional Needs Versus Physical Needs

(At this point you have scored yourself on the five characteristics that distinguish a relational/functional marriage. As a couple use your scoring for further discussion. Compare your scores as a couple with other couples by using the data that follows.)

Emotional Needs Versus Physical Needs

1. Listed below are ten important emotional needs. First, prioritize those needs. Then, on a scale of 0 to 10, score each as to how the marital partners are both aware of those needs and supportive of them.

priority of need   marital support

1. Achievement
2. Forgiveness
3. Personal growth
4. Appreciation
5. Respect
6. Support
7. Affection
8. Space
9. Play
10. Vocational growth

2. Listed below are the fruits of the Spirit (Gal. 5:22). These fruits are first produced by the presence of God in our lives. Second, they are to be shared in our marriages. Third, they direct us inward to our emotional needs.

Using the scale 1 to 10 (10 positive), evaluate the presence of each of these gifts in your own personal life. Then evaluate each of these gifts as to its presence in your marital relationship. The purpose of the exercise is to identify growth areas.

                    W   H   M

1. Love
2. Joy
3. Peace
4. Patience
5. Kindness
6. Goodness
7. Faithfulness
8. Gentleness
9. Self-control

Conclusion

The same danger that is present in polemics—exaggeration—is both subtly and obviously present in speaking and writing. In order to make a point that seems critical, needed, and valid, the temptation is to exaggerate its value in order to present it or sell it. That is certainly possible in my attempt to underscore the value of relational growth in marriage. Functional tasks are necessary, but they are not enough, nor are they sound substitutes for nurturing relational needs. Attention to the needs of the relationship is putting down roots that stabilize the marriage, so the tasks that naturally grow out of and attach themselves to the marriage and to the partners are affirmed as valid and necessary.

A well-grounded marriage is more free to face tasks responsibly and creatively. Just as the branches of a tree adorn themselves with leaves and hold fast the fruits that are produced, the roots of the tree grow down and out, seeking the nutrients that dress the branches with both foliage and fruit.

> By patient toil and judgment exquisite
>   of body, mind, and heart,
> You may, my innocents, fashion this tenderness,
>   this liking, and this passion
> Into a work of art.
>   —Jan Struther

Data

70 Couples

35 Couples from Ridgecrest Marriage Enrichment (South ern Baptist Conference and Retreat Center);
35 Marriage Enrichment Couples from Four Baptist Churches

Couples married from two weeks to fifty-two years with the average being between twelve and fifteen years.
Marriages are scored in three categories:
1. 0-10 Scale - Each of the five characteristics that distin guish a functional from a relational marriage are scored.
2. 0-50 Scale - The cumulative score on the five character istics that distinguish a functional from a relational marriage.
3. 0-50 Scale - The number of marriages that fall into the various relational-functional combinations are based on the cumulative scores of the five characteristics that dis tinguish a relational from a functional marriage.

  0 - 15 Functional
16 - 25 Functional to functional relational
26 - 35 Functional relational to relational functional
36 - 50 Relational functional to relational.

All Couples
Relational/Functional Exercise

Using the five-noted characteristics contrasting a relational and functional marriage, each marriage partner is to evaluate the marriage as relational or functional. The scale is one to ten, ten being the maximum relational. Give first your own perception of how you see the marriage, and then give your perception of how your partner sees the marriage.

Functional								Relational	
1	2	3	4	5	6	7	8	9	10

	h	w
1. Change Versus Sameness	6	6.1
2. Communication: Feelings Versus Facts	5.7	6
3. Conflict Resolution Versus Unresolved Conflict	5.6	5.7
4. Intimacy Versus Sex	6.1	6
5. Emotional Needs Versus Physical Needs	6	6.4

All Couples
(As Scored by Husbands)
Relational/Functional Exercise

Using the five-noted characteristics contrasting a relational and functional marriage, each marriage partner is to evaluate the marriage as relational or functional. The scale is one to ten, ten being the maximum relational. Give first your own perception of how you see the marriage, and then give your perception of how your partner sees the marriage.

Functional								Relational	
1	2	3	4	5	6	7	8	9	10

	h	w
1. Change Versus Sameness	5.8	5.6

2. Communication: Feelings Versus Facts   5.5   5.8
3. Conflict Resolution Versus Unresolved
Conflict   5.7   5.6
4. Intimacy Versus Sex   6.1   6.6
5. Emotional Needs Versus Physical Needs 6   6.4

All Couples
(As Scored by Wives)
Relational/Functional Exercise

Using the five-noted characteristics contrasting a relational and functional marriage, each marriage partner is to evaluate the marriage as relational or functional. The scale is one to ten, ten being the maximum relational. Give first your own perception of how you see the marriage, and then give your perception of how your partner sees the marriage.

Functional								Relational	
1	2	3	4	5	6	7	8	9	10

	h	w
1. Change Versus Sameness	6.3	6.4
2. Communication: Feelings Versus Facts	6.1	6.3
3. Conflict Resolution Versus Unresolved Conflict	5.8	6.1
4. Intimacy Versus Sex	6.2	6.3
5. Emotional Needs Versus Physical Needs	6.1	6.7

Church Couples (35)
Relational/Functional Exercise

Using the five-noted characteristics contrasting a relational and functional marriage, each marriage partner is to evaluate the marriage as relational or functional. The scale is one to ten, ten being the maximum relational.

Give first your own perception of how you see the marriage, and then give your perception of how your partner sees the marriage.

Functional								Relational	
1	2	3	4	5	6	7	8	9	10
								h	w

1. Flexibility vs. rigidity   5.9   6.4
2. Communication: feeling vs. fact   5.7   6.4
3. Conflict resolution vs. unresolved conflict5.6   5.9
4. Intimacy vs. Sex   6   6.5
5. Emotional needs vs. physical needs   6   6.7

Ridgecrest Couples (35)
Relational/Functional Exercise

Using the five-noted characteristics contrasting a relational and functional marriage, each marriage partner is to evaluate the marriage as relational or functional. The scale is one to ten, ten being the maximum relational. Give first your own perception of how you see the marriage, and then give your perception of how your partner sees the marriage.

Functional								Relational	
1	2	3	4	5	6	7	8	9	10
								h	w

1. Change Versus Sameness   6.1   5.8
2. Communication: Feelings Versus Facts   5.6   5.6
3. Conflict Resolution Versus Unresolved
Conflict   5.6   5.5
4. Intimacy Versus Sex   6.1   6.2
5. Emotional Needs Versus Physical Needs 6.   6.2

Second Marriages
(Fifteen Couples)
Relational/Functional Exercise

Using the five-noted characteristics contrasting a relational and functional marriage, each marriage partner is to evaluate the marriage as relational or functional. The scale is one to ten, ten being the maximum relational. Give first your own perception of how you see the marriage, and then give your perception of how your partner sees the marriage.

Functional								Relational	
1	2	3	4	5	6	7	8	9	10
								h	w

1. Change Versus Sameness   5.9   4.9
2. Communication: Feelings Versus Facts 6.4   6.1
3. Conflict Resolution Versus Unresolved
Conflict   4.5   5.2
4. Intimacy Versus Sex   5.9   5.9
5. Emotional Needs Versus Physical Needs 5.6   5.9

Clergy Couples
(Fifteen Couples)
Relational/Functional Exercise

Using the five-noted characteristics contrasting a relational and functional marriage, each marriage partner is to evaluate the marriage as relational or functional. The scale is one to ten, ten being the maximum relational. Give first your own perception of how you see the marriage, and then give your perception of how your partner sees the marriage.

Functional								Relational	
1	2	3	4	5	6	7	8	9	10
								h	w

1. Change Versus Sameness   6.6   6.5
2. Communication: Feelings Versus Facts 7.3   6.5
3. Conflict Resolution Versus Unresolved
    Conflict   6.4   6.

4. Intimacy Versus Sex	7.4	6.9
5. Emotional Needs Versus Physical Needs	6.6	6.6

General Scores of the 70 Couples
Total Scores: 50 points

	H.	W.
Husbands and wives' perception	29.2	
Wives and husbands' perception		30.7
Husbands only	28.5	
Wives only		30.8
Wives' perception	29.9	
Husbands' perception		30.6

35 Church Couples

	H.	W.
Husbands and wives' perception	29.0	
Wives and husbands' perception		30.6
Husbands' perception of husbands	29	
Wives' perception of wives		31.6
Wives' perception of husbands	29.6	
Husbands' perception of wives		30.4

35 Ridgecrest Couples

	H.	W.
Husbands and wives' perception	28.8	
Wives and husbands' perception		29.6
Husbands' perception of husbands	28.1	
Wives' perception of wives		29.8
Wives' perception of husbands	29.4	
Husbands' perception of wives		29.1

Scale 0 - 50

0 - 15 Functional

16 - 25 Functional to Functional Relational

26 - 35 Functional Relational to Relational Functional
36 - 50 Relational Functional to Relational

Seventy Couples

F	0 - 15	16	5%
F to FR	16 - 25	60	21%
FR to RF	26 - 35	137	49%
RF to R	36 - 50	67	25%

Scale 0 - 50

0 - 15 Functional
16 - 25 Functional to Functional Relational
26 - 35 Functional Relational to Relational Functional
36 - 50 Relational Functional to Relational

Seventy Couples: Husbands Scored Wives

F	0 - 15	5
F to FR	16 - 25	12
FR to RF	26 - 35	37
RF to R	36 - 50	16

Husbands Scored Husbands

F	0 - 15	4
F to FR	16 - 25	19
FR to RF	26 - 35	32
RF to R	36 - 50	15

Scale 0 - 50

0 - 15 Functional
16 - 25 Functional to Functional Relational
26 - 35 Functional Relational to Relational Functional
36 - 50 Relational Functional to Relational

Seventy Couples: Wives Scored Wives

F	0 - 15	2
F to FR	16 - 25	14
FR to RF	26 - 35	33
RF to R	36 - 50	21

Wives Scored Husbands

F	0 - 15	5
F to FR	16 - 25	15
FR to RF	26 - 35	35
RF to R	36 - 50	15

Scale 0 - 50

0 - 15 Functional
16 - 25 Functional to Functional Relational
26 - 35 Functional Relational to Relational Functional
36 - 50 Relational Functional to Relational

35 Church Couples

F	0 - 15	8
F to FR	16 - 25	25
FR to RF	26 - 35	69
RF to R	36 - 50	38

35 Ridgecrest Couples

F	0 - 15	8
F to FR	16 - 25	35
FR to RF	26 - 35	68
RF to R	36 - 50	29

Observations Based on Data

A study of the collected data reveals the following observations:

Wives score husbands and wives consistently higher on each of the characteristics than husbands. This reflects two tendencies. Wives tend to approach marriage more idealistically and husbands more realistically. Wives are usually assigned more responsibility for the marriage relationship and are somewhat more protective of their assignment. Wives scored husbands 29.9 and wives 30.8, while husbands scored wives 30.6 and husbands 28.5.

The one characteristic where wives scored consistently higher, both in relation to the other characteristics and to the husbands, was the value given to emotional needs. Wives were scored 6.4 over against their husbands at 6. Emotional needs were valued .3 points higher than any other characteristic.

Wives scored consistently lowest on conflict resolution. Husbands scored lowest on conflict resolution and on communicating feelings. Husbands scored highest on sexual intimacy.

Couples in second marriages scored significantly lower than couples in first marriages. This reflects more reproduction of the same in second marriages rather than learning from prior experience and change. Clergy marriages scored significantly higher than other marriages, possibly reflecting the strong need clergy marriages have to protect their marriages and to deny growth areas in their marital relationships.

Church couples scored slightly higher than the Ridgecrest (retreat setting) couples. This possibly reflects the lesser risks to couples who address and assess their marriages in a more distant setting with couples they do not know. Church couples who attend marriage enrichment, because of the higher risks, are usually stronger in their marital commitment to growth.